Mastering Negative Impulsive Thoughts

Secrets for a Longer, Happier Life!

A Powerful New Philosophy that eradicates Negative Thinking to achieve Ultimate Health, Wealth and Happiness

Dr John and Elizabeth McIntosh

Mastering Negative Impulsive Thoughts (NITs)

© 2014 GP Mx Solutions PL 2014

First published in 2014 by GP Mx Solutions

All rights reserved. No part of this publication may be reproduced, stored in a retrieval system, or transmitted in any form or by any means, electronic, mechanical, photocopying, recording or otherwise, without the written permission of the publisher.

McIntosh, Dr. John and Elizabeth

ISBN - 978-0-9924290-0-3

Listings -   1. Motivation   2. Personal Development
              3. Self Help   4. Inspirational

Contact details:
GP Mx Solutions PL
1-3 Old Eimeo Rd, Mackay, Qld
Australia 4740

Dedication

This book is dedicated to everyone who aspires to be something greater than what they are today and who has the courage to reach for the stars.

In addition we dedicate this book to all of our 'teachers' along the way – some will never know that they provided us with such inspiration and learning, but this book would not have been possible without that broad range of life experiences.

Mastering Negative Impulsive Thoughts (NITs)

Contents

	About the authors	7
	Introduction	9
1	What are Negative Impulsive Thoughts or NITs?	13
2	How can you recognise Negative Impulsive Thoughts?	25
3	Why is the source of all Negative Impulsive Thoughts FEAR?	43
4	How can you harness the power of your mind?	59
5	How do you treat your own Negative Impulsive Thoughts?	77
6	How do you treat Third Party Negative Impulsive Thoughts?	109
7	How do you create great life habits?	135
8	What about our children – the next generation?	155
9	Negative Impulsive Thoughts in intimate relationships and love	169

Contents

10	Negative Impulsive Thoughts in the workplace	193
11	Negative Impulsive Thoughts in sport	207
12	Negative Impulsive Thoughts in politics	221
13	Negative Impulsive Thoughts in religion	231
14	Negative Impulsive Thoughts in mental illness	241
15	What is the NITs-free road to success and happiness?	251
16	Where are they now?	263
17	How can you spread Negative Impulsive Thoughts awareness?	267
	Corporate programs and coaching	275
	Acknowledgements	279

About The Authors

Dr John McIntosh
MBChB, MRCP, MRCGP

Dubbed "The Medical Guru", entrepreneur Dr John McIntosh is a qualified medical doctor with specialist qualifications as a hospital physician and family doctor.

For more than 30 years, he has been a medical practitioner across four continents and is a leading educator in his field. As an international motivational speaker, regular newspaper columnist and TV and radio presenter John also runs seminars and retreats on self-development, health and wellbeing. In addition, he has also produced a series of CDs on health, relaxation and success and a TV documentary series.

Plus, he has built multi-million dollar national and international businesses from nothing, through living the philosophies he shares in this book.

John's innovative thinking has led to national awards and many new ways of delivering medical services, setting up health systems, providing community education and combining traditional and complementary services for the best outcomes. With his innovative approach to improve quality health services, he has raised the standards of medical services and is a recognised leader in his field.

Across many continents, John has also performed regular medical aid work being the team leader of expeditions to many remote islands as well as working selflessly locally and internationally in humanitarian roles.

Rev Elizabeth McIntosh BMSc

Elizabeth McIntosh is known as the "Positivity Expert" from her decades of experience and research in this field. She is qualified in Metaphysical Science, is an ordained Minister, fitness trainer, yoga and meditation teacher, Reiki Master, NLP practitioner, hypnotherapist and life coach. She is also an international motivational speaker, regular newspaper columnist, radio presenter and runs seminars and retreats on self-development, health and wellbeing. She has also produced a series of CDs on health, relaxation and success and a TV documentary series.

Elizabeth has been in clinical practice for many years and brings together her broad-based skills and personal experiences including international aid work and travel.

This results in a unique fusion of modern Western science with ancient Eastern philosophies using the best of both worlds. As a keynote, corporate and seminar presenter, she has innovative concepts to empower people to maximise their full potential and achieve Life Mastery in their personal or professional life.

As a result of years of dealing with the consequences of negative thinking in their everyday clinical practice, Dr John and Rev Elizabeth McIntosh crystalised the Negative Impulsive Thoughts (NITs) concept with effective strategies for their recognition and treatment.

Why the book Mastering Negative Impulsive Thoughts was created.

> "From the dark and lonely street,
> to the bright side of the road"
> Van Morrison

Negative Thoughts occur impulsively in every single one of us. They just pop up in our heads as part of our internal dialogue or mind chatter. How you deal with your Negative Impulsive Thoughts (NITs) will have huge effects on your physical health, success in life and emotional happiness – so your health, wealth and happiness are at stake!

Everyone has experienced thoughts of self-doubt, self-criticism and lack of self-confidence. These NITs can also keep you awake at night, create unnecessary guilt, regret or just make you feel bad in general. Other people also generate negative thoughts and comments that can dramatically impact your emotional state. Therefore, controlling NITs in yourself and from others is critical to create your future happiness and maximize your full potential.

This revolutionary new philosophy will transform every area of your life – personal, family, children, relationships, work, business and sport. You will be empowered and uplifted and be in the driver's seat on your journey to your ultimate successful life. Everyone around you will benefit as you will be an inspiration and they will learn from you these simple yet powerful techniques.

The principles of positive thinking have been well recognised for many years. However, this is the first time that negative thoughts have been simply defined and encapsulated.

Mastering Negative Impulsive Thoughts also provides a unique three-question process to recognise negative thoughts, plus an easy to follow three-step strategy for replacing NITS with positive alternatives.

Just like the head lice ("nits") that their name evokes, NITs need to be repeatedly treated and controlled. This book contains effective tools and techniques to filter out negative thoughts, stop them in their tracks, change them into positive alternatives and prevent the spread of NITs to other people. This book lifts the veil of ignorance about negative thoughts, and once aware of them, you will be amazed at their plague-like nature.

The techniques are excellent for personal development and inner contentment. It is also highly effective in managing children through their difficult times, as the challenging situations are addressed positively while maintaining a "class act". Intimate relationships will blossom as each person gives and receives freely and with abundance, resulting in the ultimate relationship. In business, these NIT-free techniques provide solutions for interpersonal conflict and workplace crises, resulting in dramatic improvement in workplace atmosphere and productivity overall.

This concept was born out of our many years of our professional experience as a medical doctor and health consultant. It became clear to us that negative thoughts are like an unrecognised epidemic that is entrenched in most people's thinking and they are often unaware of it. Unfortunately, this often has crippling results in their physical, psychological and financial achievements in their lives.

Research shows that up to 70% of visits to your family doctor arise out of negative thoughts and attitudes. Plus, studies prove that you will live nine years longer if you have a positive outlook on life. It has also been shown that this optimistic approach to life results in less heart attacks, strokes, cancers and common colds! Therefore, this is not a nebulous and fluffy subject; it is critically important for the health and wellbeing of every single one of us.

As you read this book, you will have many "Ah-hah!" moments when you are hit with new realisations and moments of enlightenment. Plus the enormity of the issue will become obvious, as it does affect every one of us personally, as well as our families, children, workplaces, schools, and our whole society. Prepare to be amazed – you have been warned!

The implications are endless, the possibilities are incredible, and happily there are solutions to solve the NITs epidemic and achieve a happier and healthier world. It all starts with YOU.

After all, as the wise saying goes:

> *"At any moment you can change your life*
> *– but what moment will you choose?"*

Let your journey to the bright side begin…

1
What Are Negative Impulse Thoughts Or NITs?

> Watch your thoughts; they become words.
> Watch your words; they become actions.
> Watch your actions; they become habits.
> Watch your habits; they become character.
> Watch your character; it becomes your destiny!
> **Lao Tzu**

Everyone's mind generates thoughts continuously. This is commonly known as your inner voice, internal dialogue or "mind chatter." It is like having a conversation with yourself, even though most people would not admit that they "talk to themselves". We establish the tone and nature of our internal dialogue from a very young age, and as we grow older, this dialogue changes according to our life experiences.

Belief in yourself is established by your successes. Your belief in your level of ability is determined by what you do and don't achieve and what feedback you get from those around you. As a child growing up, we are subjected to compliments or criticisms from our valued elders, parents, school teachers, coaches and peers. These comments will either build up your positive self-belief or implant negative beliefs which are then tested with your experiences in life. We start to establish a self belief system, which involves every aspect of our life, from our personal character to our looks, abilities, our potential future and especially our attitudes.

The saddest thing of all is that these beliefs have a huge effect on our performance and expectations in life. So if as a child, you were told that you were stupid or that you would not amount to anything, this belief will almost certainly play out as being correct when you approach any exams or learning experience with that expectation. Having internal thoughts of "I am stupid and won't do well" directly blocks the learning process. As a result, the effort of learning is reduced and of course, poor results will follow. Unfortunately, the poor results then just reinforce the incorrect belief that the person is stupid, and the vicious cycle continues.

On the other side of the coin, if you are told that you are really clever and will do great things when you grow up, your expectation of success is being cultivated. As a result, you will work harder and focus to get the right skills, and you are much more likely to get the good results that will then confirm this belief. Therefore either way, your belief system is usually a self-fulfilling prophecy. If you think you will succeed or if you think you will fail, almost always you will be right.

Typical examples of comments that affect people's self-esteem when they are young and are taken on as a truth may include:

- "You are such a naughty child."
- "Why don't you ever do as you are told?"
- "You will never amount to anything."
- "You will never be as good as your sister."
- "Pity you are not attractive like your sister."
- "You always miss the really important kicks for goal."

Clearly these comments are often made by parents, teachers or coaches with the intention of supporting the child and improving their ability. In reality, they are undermining and demoralising the young child, leading to low self-esteem and low self-belief. These simple statements, often made with little thought by the adult, can have devastating effects on the developing nature and character of the child.

These implanted beliefs are then reinforced over time to become your belief system. When you are faced with a challenge, if you believe that "you are stupid" you won't even try to do well in the test, get higher qualifications or more challenging jobs. Or when going for the vital kick to win the grand final, the voice of the coach from the Under 8 team rings through your head and you miss the kick!

Your mind chatter or internal dialogue is therefore something that has been cultivated over your entire life, influenced by your most respected teachers and reinforced by repeated events over the years. It is therefore well entrenched and deep-seated, with its roots in events and statements that you are probably not even aware of. So our first piece of advice is that changing these long-established habits will not occur overnight and will take some persistence and effort – but it CAN BE DONE!

It may be telling you:

> Mind chatter will therefore be going on inside all of us and be with most of us all the time. The big question is: what is your internal voice telling you?

- "Yes, you can achieve this goal."
- "Yes you are a great worker/beautiful/valuable asset to the company and deserve to get this job/partner/income."

Or your internal dialogue may be saying things like:

- "You always fail at this."
- "You never get the gorgeous girlfriend/boyfriend."
- "They will never give you a raise."

Mastering Negative Impulsive Thoughts (NITs)

Does your internal dialogue conjure up all the reasons why you should fail rather than succeed? Do you automatically think of all the reasons not to do something rather than the one good reason that you absolutely have to do it?

Are you basing your life and success on obsolete and negative comments about money and success? These may include:

- "He must have taken advantage of lots of people to get that rich."
- "I wonder if he can sleep at night having taken advantage of that many people."
- "Money won't make you happy."
- "Money is the root of all evil."

Of course this last one is a Bible misquote. The original actually states that the "love of money is the root of all evil." If these comments are the basis for your beliefs about success and money, it is inevitable that you will find interesting events where every time you are becoming successful, everything will fall apart as you sabotage your success.

This is because deep down you believe that:

- "Money is evil."
- "You can't be successful without ruining other people."
- "Money will make you unhappy".

Your subconscious therefore creates a stumbling block to prevent you achieving success.

This is your subconscious and mind chatter at work, and to be fair to you, it has probably had a completely free rein until today. The chances are that no-one has ever tried to make it accountable or pulled it into line, allowing the comments and self-sabotaging thoughts to flow freely and establish themselves very securely as the "status quo". You have probably had the belief that these thoughts are beyond your control, and may not even have been aware of their nature, even though every action you take has been affected by them in some way.

This is the start of the mind chatter being accountable and being brought into line with what YOU want. The negative thoughts should be scared, as we are about to start weeding them out and replacing them. In fact, right now they are probably already telling you "Ridiculous, there is no way that I can stop these thoughts!" Listen... can you hear your NITs already trying to protect the status quo? Don't worry – we will deal with them over the next few chapters.

Your mind chatter may consist of positive supportive thoughts or negative destructive thoughts. It is the negative and destructive thoughts that are the reason for this book, as they can affect our lives in such a dramatic way. NITs do seemingly occur without any conscious control, so they are "impulsive" – hence the name "Negative Impulsive Thoughts". NITs is the abbreviation, and the analogy to nits or head lice is remarkably similar.

Head lice are very contagious in the community, occur in epidemics, usually go undetected, and can only be found with careful observation. Nits are physically irritating and emotionally draining, with early treatment being most effective and multiple repeat treatments usually required. Regular monitoring is needed to ensure relapse has not occurred, and treatment of everyone in your close group should be considered if an outbreak has occurred.

Table 1   Comparison of NITs and nits (head lice)

NITs – Negative Impulsive Thoughts	Nits – Head Lice
Negative thoughts	Physical Lice
Often go unnoticed	Often go unnoticed
Not visible and only noticeable with attention	Only just visible with careful inspection and attention
Very irritating and emotionally draining	Physically irritating and emotionally draining
Infectious	Infectious
Occurring in epidemic proportions	Occurring in epidemic proportions (in third world)
Spreads rapidly through people in contact	Spreads rapidly through people in contact
Need to be recognised before treatment can be used	Need to be suspected before treatment used
Early destruction is best	Early destruction is best
Treatments are successful	Treatments are successful
Regular treatments required	Regular treatments required
Regular monitoring is necessary to prevent relapse	Regular monitoring is necessary to prevent relapse
Some Differences	
Very common problem in all ages	Common problem in children mainly
Present in <u>most</u> situations	Present mainly in schools and childcare areas
More common in developed world	Less common in developed world

What do NITs do?

> Just like the nits that are live head lice, NITs are live, irritating, spread like wildfire and keep you so occupied that you can't focus on what really needs to be done. Unless recognised and controlled, they multiply and gain strength over time until they are an unstoppable mass that overwhelms the individual, business, economy, country or religion.

NITs may start as very small doubts and, like Chinese whispers, the message changes progressively. The statement may start as "This is a bit hard", and change to "I wonder if this can be done", "This will probably fail", and finally "This is impossible – so let's just stop trying!" The classic self-fulfilling prophecy is complete and has happened before you have even tried to put effort into the challenge.

So NITs can vary from small negative doubts to major negative beliefs that are well established over time. Allowing a newly-hatched NIT to survive, like "I don't think I will be good at this new sport," leads to reinforcement every time any error is made. Plus the perception that you are "no good" becomes stronger over time. Eliminating the thought at its source and replacing it with a more positive thought will prevent the stronger negative thoughts from developing over time. For example, just saying something like "Practice makes perfect" or "Developing any skill takes persistence and I am great at persistence!" will nurture the expectation of improvement. After that, each step forward is seen as proof that you can do it and reinforces the positive thought. It also overcomes the expectation that you should get everything right first time and reinforces the need to practice. Any successful person has had to have some failures in order to learn how to do it right.

Derogatory and personal comments are also taken on board and internalised by many people. These can be accusations of being fat, thin, ugly, having a big nose, wearing glasses, being useless, worthless, a bad kisser, a bad lover or any number of personal insults. This results in poor self-image, a feeling of inadequacy and a reluctance to fully participate in life. At a performance level, you may take on comments from others about being a bad student, stupid, slow, a poor worker, a poor sales person, not being able to sing, being a bad dancer, or any number of personal beliefs. These attitudes prevent you from fully participating in life and when you do, you are not expecting success. You are likely to self-sabotage or avoid the persistent effort required for success.

In the workplace, very minor negative comments can be taken on board and result in very powerful negative beliefs about a worker's own lack of ability. This can be devastating to the worker's self-esteem, which is sometimes the desired result from a malicious workmate but is often just a thoughtless comment. The business outcomes can range from individual performance failures, lack of job satisfaction, frequent staff changes to significant reduction in profitability and/or failure of major projects.

NITs can also be directed at community-level concepts with comments such as:

- "This is such a terrible place to live."
- "We have such a high crime rate."
- "Nobody is friendly in this town."
- "It is so hard to make friends."
- "It is too hot/cold/wet/dry," etc.

Another variation of this is to compare your current place of residence with your previous ones and state how much better your previous place was. This NIT and negativity directed at the place that you have chosen to live in will not be well received by the residents, who consider that place home. As well as spreading negativity about your new home, it will also generate negativity directed at you! Think about it: the immediate thought from the locals would be to think "Well, go straight back there if it is so much better there!"

This is definitely not the way to win friends and influence people!

There are NITs that are directed at the economy of the country where negative comments are made and propagated in the media. These could be about the economy, the value of the money or about specific areas, countries, religions or safety. For example, whether the exchange rate is high or low, whether the interest rates are up or down, the reports will be negative because it creates more drama. Whether the national deficit is high or low and whether the import to export ratio is positive or negative, these will also be reported as bad by the media. You will even find the media reporting the falling unemployment rates as being a bad sign as it was "because there is an increase in the numbers of part-time workers," or other fine detail. Just listen to the tone of the media reporting on the major items. Most of it will be based on negativity, made into a logical negative argument and then forecast to the whole country.

Drama and bad news sell newspapers and magazines as well as increasing TV ratings. The evening TV news may even try to compensate with a single warm and fuzzy thirty-second story at the end of thirty minutes of intense negativity to make people feel better. These comments are often also heard from individuals in business situations and even more powerfully from politicians. Start to listen and become aware of the nature of the information that is being circulated and you will be amazed at how much is negative and how little is positive. All these influences on your subconscious affect how you think about these issues. Yet it is always amazing that the stock market falls because of an election or the dollar value falls because of unrelated events. This is all NIT-based: fear and gloom is not usually supported by reality, and values usually bounce back when the emotion passes!

The English language has three times as many terms for negative experiences as positive ones, and it is also well known that one critical comment takes ten positive comments to be negated. By recognising, understanding and treating each individual NIT, you will start:

Limiting personal NITs and therefore reduce the frequency of negative comments from you to everyone around you.

Developing the ability to recognise NITs in others and start to help control and treat them effectively too.

Hopefully, this will start to spread the understanding to people close to you and then progressively to a wider audience. The whole understanding and reduction of NITs will then multiply to create wider and more effective NIT control across your families, workplaces, communities and wider groups. As you will read in the next chapters, this NIT epidemic has affected and infected wide areas of our international community, to a level that makes the mind boggle! Solutions are available, but it needs every one of us to put in the effort, limit NITs in every situation and accept no less.

Summary

Negative Impulsive Thoughts (NITs) are very much like their namesake, head lice. They share the features of being highly contagious, spread rapidly from person to person, are difficult to recognise and need repeated treatments to eliminate them. They are like an unrecognised epidemic that is affecting almost every one of us and can affect every area of our lives with devastating effects. At a personal level, they lead to unhappiness, self-doubt, and lack of success. Plus, they also affect our children, schools, workplaces, communities and wider groups.

We must recognise and eliminate NITs because our health, success and happiness depend on it.

2
How Can You Recognise Negative Impulsive Thoughts?

> "All that we are is the result of what we have thought."
> **Buddha**

Personal NITs

The first step in dealing with NITs is to recognise them so that you will be able to eliminate them. Personal NITs is the starting point so you will need to listen to your own thoughts and words, focusing on their tone and nature. Your mind chatter or internal voice will be having a constant discussion with you about everything that is going on around you. It is assessing and judging everything that you are faced with and all decisions that you are making. How you consciously handle these thoughts will have a huge bearing on how you feel overall and how you deal with situations and people around you.

The simplest level of mind chatter is your self-image. Is your internal voice telling you that you are good or bad? Do your thoughts reinforce you as a gorgeous and a wonderful person, deserving of all the wonders that life is presenting to you? Or is your usual tone negative? Do you say that you are not attractive, don't deserve the good things in life and don't do things well so you will fail?

Your personal thoughts can also affect your perception of your relationship, family, friends, work, community and habits. These can be empowering and give you strength, or they can be NITs and erode your performance and happiness. If you have NITs about your relationship, you may think that you are not good enough for your partner or that you are no good as a husband, wife or lover. As the NITs get more severe, you may even develop doubts about fidelity and develop jealousy that can destroy the relationship.

Personal NITs are the ones that you have the most immediate control over, as they are all yours and completely in your control. We will first teach you to recognise NITs with three easy questions and then explain various tools to take control of your NITs to remove them from your mind and your life. The result is liberating and lifts you to higher levels of happiness and contentment in life, as well as removing the stumbling blocks on your pathway to higher levels of success.

Paying attention to your own thoughts will allow you learn to recognise the patterns of NITs within your own mind chatter and will then enable you to start to clean up your own act. The later step is to start trying to clean up the NITs from everyone else around you! So let's define NITs and put clear and simple boundaries around them to make them easy to recognise.

> By definition, Negative Impulsive Thoughts are negative in nature and thoughts that occur spontaneously or impulsively.

Do they empower and encourage success or are they limiting your progress and reducing your aspirations? Do you feel stronger and motivated or do you feel flat and limited? Are they encouraging action or are they creating procrastination? Are they moving you forwards and upwards or are they trapping you or even pushing you downwards? Are they allowing for the possibility of unexpected or unlimited success, or are they restricting progress based on previous bad experience? Are they putting you in a place where you might benefit from "lucky" coincidences, or are they preventing you from taking advantage of opportunities?

How Can You Recognise Negative Impulsive Thoughts?

Negative Impulsive Thoughts are:

- Negative – demeaning, denigrating, disempowering, create self-doubt or reduced expectations, poor self-image, restrictive, limiting.
- Failure-oriented – they move people away from the actions required to succeed or move forward.
- Impulsive* – they occur spontaneously and spread with ease from person to person and across communities.
- Natural – starting as thoughts, they become words and then become established as beliefs before they are accepted as the undisputed reality, often incorrectly.
- Original – they arise from within oneself, any other person, media, social media or information source.
- Circulated – worldwide (but less so in ancient spiritual cultures).
- Severe – mild to extremely damaging. May be used deliberately to undermine and disempower opponents.

---

*Please note that most negative thoughts that arise in our subconscious are impulsive. However, through the book there are also examples of people using negative denigrating statements in a deliberate manner which then create impulsive negative thoughts in others. So while these thoughts are created deliberately, the impulsive uptake and spread of them is the reason that we are still using the term "NITs" in that situation.

One warning here is that you need to make sure that you use this knowledge only for good. Having the knowledge of the power of NITs might lead you into the temptation of using them to harm others. Make sure you don't fall into this trap, as this will only bring magnified negativity back to you as the "laws of the universe" kick in and you get back what you deserve! Remember what goes around comes around.

To make the process of NIT recognition quick, easy and instantly effective in any situation, we have created three simple questions that will allow you to identify them. This allows everyone to rapidly and easily assess any thoughts, words or actions from within yourself or from external sources. These need to be memorised to be brought out in rapid fire for any situation to immediately label the NITs so you can then get into the treatment process and eliminate them.

The Magic Three Questions to identify NITs are:

- Is this information confirmed to be the truth?
- Is this information positive, empowering and uplifting to everyone concerned?
- Does this information move all concerned closer to their goals?

The answers to all three questions should obviously be "yes". This will lead you to the clear decision as to whether the information is worth bringing into your life and propagating or whether you need to suppress or eliminate the NIT. For each thought that you hear or come across, there are a number of questions you need to ask yourself about that thought:

How Can You Recognise Negative Impulsive Thoughts?

Question 1: Is the information based on the truth and confirmed as such?
Is there any doubt as to the source?
Has the information been received from both sides of the situation?

Question 2: Is it constructive or is it destructive to myself or others?
Is it helpful or unhelpful to myself and others?
Will it make me and the people around me feel good or bad?
Will it boost us up or will it cut us down?

Question 3: Is this thought going to help everyone move closer towards their goals, or is it limiting or blocking anyone in any way?
Is it helping everyone move forward, or is it slowing someone down?

For question 1, not only does the information need to be true, but it also needs to be confirmed to be true. When faced with statements where the truth is not yet confirmed, keep that information on hold for later consideration until the truth is revealed. Sometimes it is important to ask the person directly or get more specific information about the statements, like who exactly said that or believes that to be the case. What are the words that the person actually used? Get the full details of the information, preferably from the person who is meant to have said it before you jump to conclusions.

From question 2, you will be categorising them into constructive or destructive thoughts and this will give you another key as to whether the items are NITs or not. It will give you clues as to whether you should act on this thought, let the thought turn into words and actions or dismiss the thought.

Question 3 relates to the issue of whether the thought moves you closer to your goals or further from the goals. This particular question helps recognise information that may be the truth but is going to be detrimental or unhelpful for yourself or others. There are many truths that will clearly be moving you away from the goal. They may have passed through the second question relating to being constructive by being camouflaged with a veneer of a compliment. However, on closer inspection, it was really a damaging NIT.

Gossip, sarcasm and innuendo are usually not based on the truth so they will definitely fail the first question as well as failing both question 2 and 3. Many problems will be created if you react emotionally to gossip so all these types of comments need to be immediately recognised as NITs so they can be effectively treated.

You will need to practice your skills at NIT recognition so that it becomes a habit that you have in place all the time. You could compare this to a hair net to prevent nits from getting out or a virus filter on your computer. The NIT filter needs to be active and turned on at all times. This will ensure that any destructive and infectious NITs are recognised immediately within your own head and when coming from others. As your NIT awareness grows, you will start to recognise them in your family, friends, work colleagues, your business, your community, your religious and political leaders… and these are the people leading us!

> Make it a priority to protect yourself first, then we will show you how to work outwards to start eliminating NITs from your family, your work, your community, your leaders and hopefully then the whole world. But as Michael Jackson sang in his award winning song, *"The Man in the Mirror"*, if you want the world to change, it all starts with YOU. We encourage you to listen to this song again or read the lyrics online.

Examples of self sabotaging NITS

We have seen many examples of self sabotaging NITS in our clinical practice. Many people come to us repeatedly trying to diet, starting to lose weight and then crashing out. What has happened is that the actions of improved diet and exercise start to have their predictable effects of weight loss. However, because the self-image of the person is that they are unworthy and not really sexy or attractive, they return to their bad habit of over-eating. As a result, their poor self-image returns them to that overweight state. This is an example of self-sabotaging NITs.

Clive

Another example is partners of successful people who unconsciously sabotage their marriages as they feel unworthy of being with a person "above their standing" – richer, more attractive or of a higher status. This was the case with Clive, who was tall, dark and handsome and one of the best-looking guys in high school. He performed well at sports and academically and fell in love with the prettiest girl at school. At school he was voted as the person most likely to succeed and seemingly had everything going for him. After a few years their relationship grew, they married and it appeared to be a match made in heaven. Most handsome guy at school marries most gorgeous girl.

Underneath the surface, this handsome man had been criticised by his very negative father all his life, with comments like:

- *"Don't get too big for your boots; you are nothing special."*
- *"You'll fall flat on your face if you try to be more than what you are."*
- *"Know your place in life; you don't want to rub shoulders with those stuck-up rich &%$#s!"*

Mastering Negative Impulsive Thoughts (NITs)

The success option was destroyed for Clive throughout his childhood with repeated derogatory references:

- *"The rich only get there by cheating."*
- *"We are happy without all that flash stuff – it doesn't make you happy."*
- *"How many people did those big dealers rip off to get wealthy?"*

On top of that, there were also bad attitudes to women, which also spilled out later in Clive's relationship. Clive's low self-esteem was reflected in the comments that he made to his gorgeous wife, like:

- *"I am not worthy of you – you will probably leave me for someone better!"*

Despite her efforts in trying to build up his self-confidence and telling him how wonderful he was and how much she loved him, the implanted poor self-esteem constantly eroded his ability to enjoy the relationship. His subconscious negative view towards success showed itself over time as they built and sold houses but he would never allow them to keep the properties for long enough to build in value. Unwilling to carry the debt, properties were sold in poor market times and he continuously sabotaged their potential success with similar poor business decisions. He would have been a multi-millionaire over twenty years, if he had just kept the houses that they built and rented them out with the rent paying the mortgages and the asset values doubling every 7-10 years.

His poor self-esteem pervaded his marriage, and his belief that he "was not worthy" of this beautiful woman, progressively created situations and attitudes that were intolerable. This included wild jealousy, overbearing control of everything, dictating what she was allowed to do and who she was allowed to talk to. He also structured their life so that she was being belittled, demeaned and not valued.
Of course, there is only so much anyone will take and his wife became increasingly emotionally isolated, unloved and denigrated. His repeated statements of "I am not worthy of you," became a reality as

his whole life was sabotaged by the pre-existing beliefs and attitudes that originally came from his father. Twenty years after getting married, they divorced with almost no assets, and what should have been a fairytale life of the best guy and girl at high school became a sad statistic and another court case.

So, for all the mothers and fathers out there: take note that what you say to your children has a huge impact on every aspect of their lives.

While this is an example of what can happen in your personal and financial life as a result of unrecognized and unchecked NITs, people have also been known to actively perform inappropriate actions in good jobs so that they were fired, as their underlying belief was that they were not worthy of that position. Interestingly, in all these situations, the other parties were often happy with the individuals. However, it was the individuals themselves who felt unworthy and these beliefs were based on NITs from their own subconscious – strong examples of their thoughts controlling their life.

Minor NITs can act a bit like drips on a calm pond of water, causing disturbances that build up over time. A single unsubstantiated comment can gain momentum, causing increasing disharmony and chaos. This can affect your relationship, your workplace or yourself personally. It is not necessarily the initiator of a minor NIT that creates the larger problem, as some people will take the information and embellish it, magnify it and spread it further with the resulting storm of potentially untrue information. The original comment may have been an innocent comment or thought, not intended to be taken as anything more significant, but the damage in the long term can be huge. People do make a lot of off-the-cuff statements without any filtering for accuracy or appropriateness, and this certainly creates a lot more damage than they realise.

Daisy

In one business, one staff member behind the reception desk was chatting to her co-worker, discussing the opposition clinic, and in the conversation Daisy said that the other business "runs rings around this place!" The first ripple effect was the other receptionists at the desk feeling very uncomfortable and unsettled with the conversation, making them doubt the quality of the services that they were involved with. The comment gave them the impression that they were not doing a good job personally. These receptionists then discussed with other workers about how the other business "does such a better job" and so all the staff were affected. Being at the front desk, clients were within earshot of the comment. So the effects flowed outwards to the clients, with those clients hearing this information from a "reliable source" within the business. It is anyone's guess what they then said to their friends or associates when they were asked what the business was like.

The ripple effect flowing outwards is enormous. Word of mouth is often the most effective way to build a reputation, but you need the reputation being spread to be a good one and not a bad one! This comment also undermined the owners of the business and the quality of the business overall. Daisy also showed complete disrespect and disloyalty to the business that was paying her wages and reflecting the assumption that the staff in the business were not providing the best service that could be offered. This single comment is exactly the sort of comment that needs to be eliminated before the thought gets to become words.

If challenged, the person in Daisy's position may well say:

- *"Oh no I did not mean that – I was just joking."*
- *"No, I was just having a bad day!"*
- *"I was just referring to the extra services that the other business does and was not meaning that they provide better services at all!"*

Well, that person's bad day has had a ripple effect, giving many other people a bad day as well, and a huge negative effect on the business – which may in fact be your business one day!

Jonathon
Another good example of the ripple effect occurred in one of our practices where a relatively new doctor to the country misunderstood a comment from an official in a government department about the process of teaching medical students and unregistered doctors. The issue was whether the student was allowed to perform a consultation with the patient alone before the registered doctor took over to assess the patient and decide on the investigations and treatment. Unfortunately, the way he explained it to the official made it sound like the students were performing the whole consultation alone without any registered doctor input.

Consequently, the official said that it was "illegal" and this doctor immediately stormed to the front desk in the public waiting room of the practice and stated in front of all the receptionists and several patients that "This practice is operating illegally and I will not be associated with any illegal processes!" Suddenly we had patients, receptionists and all the other doctors labouring under the belief that something illegal was going on, and there was widespread concern! After several weeks of active negotiation and "putting out the fires", all the damaging NITs were eradicated, the staff and doctors were fully informed and settled down. Plus, the official was also informed of the actual processes that were in place, in keeping with standard teaching practice.

Of course, it would have been more appropriate for that doctor to approach the practice manager or senior medical partner to discuss what they had been told. In that way the information could have been corrected before the damaging outburst occurred. Unfortunately, a single one-sentence, twenty-second outburst of a very powerful NIT, inappropriately released in a public waiting room, caused damaging ramifications that had to be dealt with unnecessarily. Getting confirmation of the information by asking the three magic NIT questions would have stopped this outburst too. This situation was more than a ripple effect, though: it felt like a full-blown tsunami!

So the lesson here is to get all the information accurately before you have an emotional reaction. As the wise old saying advises: "Respond, don't react."

Gossip and NITs

Gossip will usually fall into the NIT category, as it is unsubstantiated, mostly negative and may be used as light relief for people without enough drama in their own lives. Obviously trying to differentiate the truth from gossip is difficult. However, the tone of the information, the source and the amount of balance of information from both sides will be good clues as to whether the information is true or not. Remember even if the information is true, if it is not uplifting and empowering for all involved, it is still a NIT! If you allow yourself to be drawn into the NITs of gossip, you will pull yourself down in the longer term.

Examples abound of gossip in almost every group, and the underlying motivation may be malice, boredom or just pure bloody-mindedness. The gossip-spreader is looking for drama and an "Oh, my God!" response. Probably every single one of us has experienced malicious gossip aimed at us in the past and the comments may be personal, business related, about our reputation or ethics. The attacks can come from any direction, and if one set of accusations fail to have the desired response, the direction may change so you can end up trying to defend different aspects of your life consecutively. After relationship breakdowns, this is very common with often every aspect of your life being attacked. Gossip or denigration may be an attempt to reduce your success if you are being seen to be getting ahead.

Malicious NITs

NITs may also be used deliberately and maliciously by someone for their own benefit in some way while being detrimental to yourself or others. It could be the deliberate spreading of rumours (NITs) about bad behaviour, bad attitude, poor performance or abilities. NITs that are spread behind people's backs are hard to deal with as the source is not always clear.

Keeping your NIT radar active and passing the information through the NIT filter of the magic three questions should allow you to decide if it is a NIT and if you will accept or reject this information. It is certainly very important that when you come across a NIT, you do not allow it to propagate further by spreading it to others. One option here is to acknowledge the potential of the facts being wrong with a comment like "I am not sure if it is true, so let's wait until we get confirmation of that before we jump to conclusions." Another option is to say "That certainly doesn't sound like the Jo that I know. I think we should wait and see if that is the truth before jumping to conclusions."

Situational NITs

Situational NITs are when the negative comments are directed at the situation you are in at the time. It may be that the comments are directed at some aspect of a business, club, sport, restaurant, meeting or event.

These comments will create negative expectations from all involved and this often results in the event or situation failing. If you are at a restaurant and expect poor service, you will be looking for faults with the service, your manner will be negative, creating defensive behaviour from the staff and the service levels will probably fall. If someone states that "nothing will come out of this meeting", the negative expectation leads to lack of effort to find resolutions and a downward spiral follows.

It is amazing that with an open mind and absence of judgment, you can learn remarkable things in the worst situations and from the worst teachers. We can also learn from the most disadvantaged or disabled people who may be having absolutely wonderful times, oblivious to our concerns. It is definitely possible to turn a potentially awful experience into a wonderful one – but it is all up to YOU to look for the opportunity, hilarity, learning experience or issue arising out of the situation.

As the wise saying goes: "There is opportunity in every catastrophe!"

"Always, Never, Everyone, No-one" usually = NITs

This is another breed of NITs, with broad statements using the above terms by definition making them incorrect. So anytime you hear someone using the terms "always, never, everyone and no-one" with negative intent, it will usually mean that you are dealing with a NIT! It is a common strategy to embellish an argument with these terms to make the other party seem so out of touch that they must be wrong, because "everyone" agrees with this, "no-one" is on your side, you are "always wrong", etc.

Many of us have fallen for this self-indulgent negativity, especially when we feel overwhelmed. Even though it may have felt like this at the time, when we make statements like these we are usually wrong. Even if these statements are true some of the time, saying "always" or "never" makes them untrue.

Going through the higher levels of specialist exams where the multiple choice questions asked for a true or false answer, I was always very much happier when faced with a question including an "always" or a "never", as they were almost always wrong!

When dealing with NITs, these key words will now make you prick up your ears. We encourage you to ask a few more questions, even if it is only in your head, as you will be finding NITs galore in the "always, never, everyone, no-one" statements.

Camouflaged NITs and Mixed Messages

There are a variety of comments and thoughts that sound positive but are actually NITs in disguise. These thoughts and comments have a positive slant but are based on a negative belief or focus on a negative aspect of life or the situation.

Typical examples of camouflaged NITs are:

- "You are looking good for someone of your age."
- "That's a lovely dress; I used to have one like that years ago."
- "You are a great nurse so keep to that and avoid management issues."
- "Great singing, but keep your day job!"

There will be some situations where a thought or process will have good effects for some people or some areas, but have a negative impact in other areas. If this is the case, then the thought or message that is put out must be modified to avoid being a NIT, as the negative impact will gain power and potentially overwhelm the positive energy and your good intention.

The message needs to be modified so that the negative aspect is avoided and only the positive message is conveyed. For example, you would avoid comments like "You are so much better than the other staff" as it has NIT-like qualities for the "other staff." A suitable alternative approach is to compliment the whole team with personal extra praise for the intended recipient: "We are very fortunate to have such a great team that works so well together. Your (be specific) leadership skills and dedication really are an inspiration to the other staff. We really appreciate all the hard work and extra effort you are putting in".

Another example may occur when you are teaching and the student is performing something incorrectly. "You are doing that incorrectly and you need to do it like this," may not be taken well by the student. A better approach would be to compliment the student on how well they are doing in one area and make a suggestion. "One thing that will improve your performance even more is to try… and see if that works better for you".

It is always good to then reinforce the original compliments about other areas that the student is performing well in and this way you are "sandwiching" the behaviour modification suggestion between two complimentary comments.

Summary

Negative Impulsive Thoughts affect every single one of us, and recognising them is the start of the process in their elimination. The Three Magic Questions will allow you to determine whether thoughts, actions or words fall into the NIT category: is this confirmed to be the truth? Is this positive, empowering and uplifting to everyone concerned? Does this move all concerned closer to their goals?

NITs fall into categories of personal, second party, third party, situational, malicious, and camouflaged, but the most important ones to deal with are the ones that are in your own head!

What do you need to do to deal with them when you find them? Read on, as all will be revealed...

3

Why Is The Source Of All Negative Impulsive Thoughts Fear?

> "The only thing we have to fear is fear itself."
> **Franklin D. Roosevelt**

Before addressing the large issue of treating Negative Impulsive Thoughts we must give you some background information about the underlying reasons for NITs and why they are being created. Interestingly, once you peel back all the layers of camouflage that cover the NITs, the emotion at the source of all of them is fear. Frequently the fear is obvious, but in some instances the fear may be buried under excuses or false logic. However, once those layers are stripped away, the fear causing the NITs becomes obvious to you.

Once you can recognise NITs for what they are, you may be able to identify the fear underlying them. It will then become much easier to deal with the NITs so they have no power over you and this is especially important when dealing with NITs from other people.

Second and third party NITs are the ones spread by other people that you will commonly hear in "normal" conversations. These NITs may be completely untrue or partially untrue and they are derogatory towards the subject, resulting in a negative impact and are destructive in some way.

When you start to look at the NITs that others throw around, there will usually be some underlying motivation for this action.

Mastering Negative Impulsive Thoughts (NITs)

These may include:

- mindless gossip
- personal retribution
- personal power issues
- desire to undermine the subject
- an attempt to make themselves feel better by highlighting the "failures" of someone else.

Obviously, these second and third party NIT-slingers are functioning from a low emotional level because their own self-esteem is based on their need to cut someone else down. This is sad, both from the perspective of the person in this low-level place and from the perspective of the damage that they cause with their NITs.

The most common source of NITs comes from a fear of failure, e.g. "I am not good enough." These fears are often easy to spot once we take a moment to identify them. The fears that underpin the NITs coming from second and third parties are very commonly camouflaged with other layers such as humour, sarcasm, quality concerns or superiority. Yet when you work down through the layers, fear is always the cause.

A work example might be the colleague who is putting out NITs about your work ability, performance or efficiency and is afraid that you may get the next promotion rather than them. If your work performance is clearly and visibly better than theirs, they would probably lower themselves to creating NITs about your non-work related issues e.g. appearance, love life, hobbies, habits or friends.

Please remember that if this is happening, it is actually a good sign that those individuals are desperate to say something bad about you. However, as they can't find anything negative in your work performance, they have to move to other areas of your life.

Why Is The Source Of All Negative Impulsive Thoughts FEAR?

Other examples are when NITs are created by your direct competitors about your business or services offered. Experience has shown us that when your business services show clear improvements over the competition, the NITs start flying as they are fearful at two main levels: the first one is that you may take business away from them, but even when their business is not under threat, their standards are now seen to be lower than others so it makes their business look poor.

This fear of being shown up is also present at a personal level, and is the basis of the Tall Poppy Syndrome. Once you start appearing to be a better or a more successful person than the average person in your field, others may start to feel inadequate. But instead of celebrating your improvements or striving to improve their service, the common reaction is to try and cut you back down to their level. What a waste of energy!

Unfortunately, as you continue to grow and achieve more success you may find the NITs and personal attacks become stronger, more vindictive and less based on truth. For those people who are striving for success just be aware of this potential situation. Remember the people who support and encourage you are the ones that you want to include in your network. Those that are critical and try to pull you down need to be excluded, as that negative influence, even if very subtle, will instill doubts and fears in you and your supporters so your success would be more difficult.

Elizabeth: *An example of a third-party NIT created from personal inadequacy was when a relative openly stated at a family gathering that she "knew for a fact that Elizabeth had an affair because she told me this in confidence!" Of course, all listening believed this to be the truth, although this person subsequently admitted to only one person that it was a completely fabricated lie without any substance.*

When asked why she did it, she replied that she "wanted to see Elizabeth's parents shocked at her behaviour as they held her on a pedestal and believed that she could do no wrong and she wanted to bring her down a peg or two." Fortunately, as the years rolled on, the family generally realised the truth. Yet there were serious repercussions for several years and my father died before the truth was revealed.

John: Another example of personal NITs occurred when I went off on a six months sailing trip to the remote islands of New Caledonia and Vanuatu. This trip was a personal dream of mine that I had been planning and manifesting for many years, and was the result of a lot of hard work and persistence. During the trip, I provided medical aid work, helped to build aid posts on remote islands and spent a lot of time teaching health workers how to treat the different illnesses with the medications that were available to them. This was with an aid program called Project MARC (Medical Assistance to Remote Communities), and I came across them by chance in the outer Islands of Vanuatu. Along with the cultural experience, the wonderful coral, beaches, fish and islands, the whole trip was an amazing experience.

On returning home, I was met with a wide array of NITs about my personal activities including wild orgies on the boat, womanising, and apparently that I had been stealing goods from the villagers' huts! Of course, anyone who knows these Melanesian islands and their culture would know that with the strict missionary indoctrination over the centuries, all the women wear "Mother Hubbard" dresses and are extremely modest, even wearing these long dresses when they swim! A sexual relationship in this community would be culturally unacceptable and require marriage.

Not to mention that the level of sexually transmitted diseases was so high that personal risk would prevent such activity. However, those were the NITs that were being circulated by both personal and professional contacts in my home town.

The visible outer layers of the NITs are social outrage that a successful person and doctor could behave in this socially unacceptable manner. Peel back a layer, and you see that by denigrating my reputation,

Why Is The Source Of All Negative Impulsive Thoughts FEAR?

the other doctors in town are able to recruit extra business for themselves and it should be noted that this is despite any criticism of any professional ineptitude.

Peel back another layer, and we start to see the anger that these professionals felt about me having the audacity to take six months off work and go off on a sailing holiday, even if they didn't like sailing. How dare this person just leave and have the ability to organise his life to enjoy himself so much?

Go down yet another layer, and you start to see that my ability to take off this time reflects badly on them personally, because if I can do it, why can't they? How do they answer their spouse when he or she asks "Well, if he can take six months off work, why can't we?" The fear of being shown up as being a lesser person, lesser professional or less lucrative business owner are all shown to be the core fears of this group, but it is all hidden under the veneer of indignation, criticism and sarcastic comments.

So remember when you start to rise above the average or status quo, non supportive people will use NITs to try and bring you back down to the average level. Plus, if they had their way, they would pull you down even further to be below average. As you become progressively more and more successful, the NITs become proportionately more aggressive, desperate and unrelated to the issue at hand. You have been warned!

When you start getting these kinds of NITs thrown at you, the usual reaction to this unfair treatment is anger and retaliation. You may lash out at those responsible in an equally derogatory or degrading manner, with personal insults then being slung back and forth. Be warned, this is exactly the response that the NIT-slingers are looking for. You have just lowered yourself to their level of functioning, and they have smugly pulled you down to their level. This is exactly the breeding cycle that keeps NITs multiplying. Plus, the NIT-slinger is able to add fuel to the NIT wildfire by embellishing the story now by adding that you have personally been attacking them and said "this" or done "that."

Keep your emotions cool, and never show any anger or negative emotion. Correct the errors in what has been stated without any personal references about the other people, and if possible make light or humour of such "ridiculous" statements. If you can, state that "they are so far from reality that they don't even require a response!" Remember, it is really hard to prove a negative like "I didn't do it", "I didn't say that" or "I am not a womaniser."

Therefore, pushing harder and harder and showing your annoyance just proves to the NIT-slingers that they are getting to you – so they will keep on going. Laugh at it, hold your head high, maintain a "class act" with integrity and let the future do your talking for you. Time will prove the level of functioning that you are at. The NIT slinger will continue to behave in their negative way repeating similar accusations to other successful people. Yet their surroundings will be a reflection of their own negative attitudes or karma. Leave them to it. Live well and maintain your integrity!

The fear that underlies any NITs that you create is often direct and usually easily recognisable as long as you are honest with yourself. Sometimes, though, you may have deeper fears generating NITs that may be conscious or subconscious. Even if you can't find out the actual reason why you produce the NITs, you do need to focus on recognising them. Next step is to treat the NITs that you have created and prevent yourself from creating any more NITs.

Trying to work out what is the underlying motivation for second and third party NITs is sometimes very difficult, even when you are the subject of them. It can be that even the NIT-slinger doesn't consciously understand their real motives and will never admit to it anyway. Remember the wise saying "The other person's opinion is private and none of your business."

Don't waste your time and emotional energy trying to work it out – just deal with the NITs in the ways we are about to show you and move onward and upward with your life. The NIT-slinger may learn better approaches in life, or they may not – they will reap their harvest either way. What goes around comes around – karma will do its work without any input from you.

Obviously NITs that have been spread about you (or anyone else) prevent the truth about your skills or personal virtues being evident and visible. With a pre-existing negative concept put out about a subject, people will look for evidence that it is correct and block the positive qualities from being noticed. So a comment like "He/she is so controlling," will create that expectation, and people will be focused on watching for that character trait. The positive traits of generosity, openness, kindness and honesty will often go unnoticed as a result.

Examples of third party accusations may include:

- "Be careful because he is such a womaniser!"
- "You can't trust him/her in business."
- "He/she will take advantage of you."
- "He/she is really terrible to work for."

These kinds of statements are impossible to contradict in the short term. How long must you wait before a NIT like these can be forgotten or proven false? Proving that you will never do something takes a long time, and the NIT slingers are skilled at spreading the NITs that are impossible to disprove.

> While it is nice to be able to work out the underlying reasons for second and third party NITs, it is not worth your time and effort – just get rid of them!

Personal Fear – What Are the Benefits?

While fear is the underlying reason for creating the NITs, fear itself is not necessarily a bad emotion. Like stress, fear creates an automatic physical and emotional response in all of us, and this response has been critical to our survival over millions of years of evolution. It is not, therefore, a bad thing at all; we just need to make the right choices when faced with it.

Everyone regularly experiences fear, and the way the body automatically responds to fear is with the fight-or-flight reaction. Adrenaline is produced, which increases the pulse, dilates the arteries to your muscles and brain and diverts blood away from the non-essential organs, like the skin and gut. The nerve connections are **stimulated**, pumped and ready, while the sugars and fats are released ready to be used in the physical action expected as you fight or run. The heightened performance of the brain allows you to think, remember and solve problems faster. This can help with speeches, exams, important business meetings and with physical performance if you are competing. This reaction has saved our lives and probably our species, so it is not intrinsically bad.

There are two provisos that we would include here:

- This stress or fear reaction should not be with you all the time, as it puts excess strain on your heart, keeps the sugar and cholesterol levels high. It is important for you to burn off this energy with vigorous exercise otherwise it can be bad for you.

- How you react to this fear is what is important: if it prevents you doing what you really need to do or if you react to the fear and generate widespread malicious NITs, then you need to develop alternative reactions to the situation.

Why Is The Source Of All Negative Impulsive Thoughts FEAR?

This is a learned skill that can be done by anyone. Obviously, there are several high-adrenaline "fun" activities that are purely based on fear. These include mountain-climbing, bungee-jumping, sky-diving, base-jumping, adventure sports and motorbike riding. Whether you think these are great fun or ridiculously high-risk activities, these are just different reactions, with some finding it exciting and some finding it to be their worst nightmare. "Feel the fear and do it anyway" is the motto for many of these sports, and controlling your reaction to the fear is part of the satisfaction of completing the task.

__John__: A lovely example of not letting fear overcome your actions was seen on another trip to Vanuatu, when again we were doing aid work, but this time as the senior doctor, leading a team of doctors providing medical services. We were based on one of the remote islands of Sakau, about to have breakfast of herbal tea made from local flowers (caffeine-free and taste-free too), boiled rice and coconut jam served on a banana leaf on the floor of the chief's straw hut. Our children knew that whatever we were offered, they needed to eat, as there was nothing else coming later, so we were all gratefully enjoying island life. At this point, we saw someone running along the beach and knew instantly that something serious was wrong because no-one ever runs in these islands except in an emergency. The young man was calling out "Dr John, Dr John!" As we ran to meet him, we found out that his wife was in advanced labour and had just spent the last four hours paddling over to Sakau from a neighbouring island, knowing that I was there.

It turned out that this was the first child for Mia and from the large eyes and the fast breathing, she was clearly in distress and terrified from obstructed labour. There is a high rate of stillbirth and maternal deaths from complicated labour in these isolated areas. We carried her along the beach to the aid post that we had built, rock by rock, the previous year, so I knew the place well. Here there was privacy, a dry roof, and clean floors with the most basic of equipment: gloves, scissors and suturing material.

Mastering Negative Impulsive Thoughts (NITs)

At least here we had some protection from the elements and the mosquitoes, and if procedures were needed, they could be done better here than in the straw huts of the village.

Mia was suffering, as was evident from her expressions, but at no point in the whole process did she cry out or scream in agony. Her baby had become impacted and was not advancing as it should, so manual assistance to manipulate the baby's head was going to be required. With limited Bislama language, I explained that the baby's head was stuck in the birth canal.

Mia seemed to understand exactly what I meant and was agreeable and nodding when I gesticulated that we needed to twist the head around to allow it to come out. Her big brown eyes were wide and frightened, but she trusted me and knew that there was no other way. From my perspective, having no back-up and knowing that I had to sort this or both mother and baby could be lost, I knew that it was completely up to me. I was the best hope that she had, even though it had been at least fifteen years since my last delivery.

This was not a time to let fear and NITs interfere with the job at hand. Admittedly, she probably had more confidence in my ability than I did – after all, I was a physician and family doctor, not an obstetrician. But to Mia, a doctor was a doctor and this was what they did! So that was what I had to do, and we both had to banish NITs and overcome the fear.

The internal examination did reveal crowning or jamming of the baby's head in the pelvic bones, so it had to be pushed back up between contractions and then rotated around into the correct position. Not having the advantage of the usual instruments that would normally make this procedure easier just meant more persistence was required from all of us. Our plan included staying calm and some trial and error as I manipulated the slippery head around with my fingers. All of this was done without Mia having any drugs or anaesthetics of any kind and by the light of some hurricane lamps.

Why Is The Source Of All Negative Impulsive Thoughts FEAR?

The other thing that came to light during this time was that Mia had the belief that it was better to lie on her back to give birth "as this was how the missionaries taught them." Because the island way of crouching in childbirth had thereby been made taboo, the complication rates and difficulties in childbirth had increased.

With our assistance, she happily adopted the traditional crouch pose, where gravity helps the mother drop the baby out and the diaphragm and chest can be used to greater effect to help with the birth. It is also the case that the islanders have quite a pronounced curve forwards in their lower spine, which is accentuated by lying down, causing an additional obstruction to the passage of the baby.

After changing positions, Mia progressed nicely through the last few stages of delivery, apart from the umbilical cord needing to be unwrapped from around the baby's neck. The only sound made by Mia during the whole delivery was a breathing gasp with the final push. Finally, with the baby lying safely in our arms, taking that first breath, having good colour and a wonderfully strong cry that echoed through the village, we all let out a huge sigh of relief.

The important thing is to focus on what you need to do and what you can do, and never let NITs take your focus off the goal at hand. Mia knew that she needed help, so while having contractions every 20-30 seconds, she'd paddled in a dug-out canoe for hours to get to me. I had to delve deep into my obsolete memory banks for obstetric information to get her to successfully deliver. Plus, both of us had to focus and persist at getting the job done. The adverse consequences were not worth considering, and the focus needed to be a successful NIT-free delivery. The baby was successfully delivered with no complications, and after a good night's sleep, Mia and her husband happily paddled back to their island with their baby in their arms.

Elizabeth: *Another experience where panic and fear would have had a potentially catastrophic effect was when I was faced with being in a lightning storm crossing over from one Indonesian island to another* in a small wooden boat. The trip was dangerous enough in itself, with the added risk that the boat was carrying multiple twenty-litre jerry cans of petrol with no caps and only plastic bags shoved into the hole acting as lids.

As the thunderstorm enveloped the boat, the waves picked up, making the ride very rough and sliding the jerry cans all around the boat, threatening to topple over and splash the petrol around the boat. To prevent this, I wedged myself into the bottom of the boat, trying to stop the cans from moving as the lightning strikes crashed out of the sky, landing on the water around the boat. Smelling fuel and feeling surprisingly wet with my skin stinging, I looked down only to see that I was dripping in petrol, which was slopping and splashing out of the can all over my back and chest.

"Not a great combination, petrol and lightning," I thought. Off came my jumper to reduce the volume of petrol on my body and I knew that here was a situation that was completely reliant on chance or fate – it all depended where the lightning hit. Nothing to be done, no action that could change the events, so no need to panic or fear as it would not do any good. In reality, petrol or no petrol, a lightning strike in an open boat at sea would make little difference to the outcome. Clearly the gods were kind that day and I lived to share the tale!

Don't Take Yourself Too Seriously

If there is one lesson we wish we could have learned earlier, it is to lighten up and not take everything so seriously! Our observations of human behaviour over the years and our personal challenges have led to the belief that we, as a civilisation generally take ourselves far too seriously. We know that many of the situations that we thought of as catastrophic at the time had ways of sorting themselves out. The people in the situations that we were very worried about, learned lessons along the way and pulled themselves out of it anyway.

On the other hand, people make their own self-destructive decisions in life against the advice you give and this is disappointing when you know where this path will lead. We need to have the wisdom to recognise that certain things are outside of our control and allow others to choose their own path. However, the important thing here is to make sure that it is them (and not you) that pays the price for these decisions. Let it go, don't take it on board and don't let those negative thoughts of potential bad outcomes into your emotional state.

> One way of allowing yourself to lighten up is to look at life like a game that we participate in and need to enjoy along the way. Experience and fully participate in every turn, twist and challenge that comes your way while remembering that you can't take it with you – you just need to enjoy the journey.

Remember that other people's NITs reflect the level at which they are operating, so don't let other people's NITs bring you down or cause you to take things too seriously. Like a game, you might have the ball under your arm heading for the try line, but your opponents are doing their best to keep you from touching-down. With any game, success comes from overcoming the struggles, and dealing with the opposition. NITs may come at you from surprising quarters and even from the people that love you! Your success is determined by having a great attitude, enjoying the "game of life" and its unpredictable little surprises, and how adaptable you are to change. So lighten up!

Mastering Negative Impulsive Thoughts (NITs)

At the end of every day, when you look over the day's activities, we encourage you to reflect on how you played the game of life today:

- What did I do well?
- What did I enjoy the most?
- Did I play with integrity and compassion?
- Am I proud of my performance today?
- What are the things I can enjoy more tomorrow?
- Am I on track with the wonderful game of life, or am I being sidetracked by others into not enjoying the game as much as I could?

Enjoy the journey...

Summary

Underlying all NITs is fear. Be honest with yourself and recognise the source of the fear, as this will start to resolve it. If you can't find the reason, just deal with the NITs anyway. Don't waste your emotional energy as the reason will come to you over time.

Similarly with second and third party NITs, if the underlying fear is not obvious, don't waste your emotional energy trying to find it, just protect yourself from the NITs and move onward and upwards. "The other person's opinion is none of your business."

Don't take yourself too seriously. Treat life like an enjoyable game to be played the best that you can and remember to have fun! Your future will be determined by what you think, what you do and who you have around you. So choose well.

4

How Can You Harness The Power Of The Mind?

> "The only limitations in life are
> the ones that you place on yourself."
> **Kristinna Habashy**

It is important that you understand just how your mind works so that you can use this information to more successfully control NITs. This knowledge will also show you how there are proven processes to harness the power of your mind to feel fantastic and full of energy, achieve levels of success way beyond what you would think possible, and most importantly achieve happiness and contentment. Annihilation of NITs is required to achieve all of this!

In this chapter, we will explain some of the medically proven principles of:

- The physiology of your brain.
- How your brain changes in response to positive and negative thoughts.
- How the Universal Law of Attraction operates.
- Plus share the secrets of the journey to success.

In order to harness the power of your mind and attract success, we need to explore the mysterious workings of the mind, the magnetic power of thought and universal principles of life. These concepts are well established and used in clinical practice by harnessing what you think to achieve preferred outcomes in your life and a better reality. These principles form the basis of many human behaviour treatments and self-mastery. Elite athletes widely use these techniques as they strive for superiority in their field, because they are known to be effective to improve performance and create more successful outcomes.

The elite athlete will visualise themselves performing the activity in their mind over and over again with perfection and the victorious outcome. They will feel, with strong emotion, what it is like to cross the line first or stand on the podium with their country's national anthem playing as they receive their gold medal. They will have rehearsed the whole event in their mind so many times, that by the time the event occurs, they already know how they are going to perform and what the outcome will be. They therefore perform to that expectation and are more likely to have the visualised outcome and win!

There have been many books written about the Law of Attraction including:

- Napoleon Hill's, *Think and Grow Rich*
- Jack Canfield's, *Principles of Success*
- Esther and Jerry Hicks', *The Law of Attraction and many others*

The fundamental underlying principles are the same, with the power of thought able to create either positive or negative effects in your life. These principles are confirmed in clinical practice as we see individuals developing cancer after very stressful events or the death of a spouse, even though no underlying medical condition exists. On the positive side, there are cases of diagnosed cancers mysteriously disappearing in individuals who focus their positive energy on healing themselves. People have managed to walk again despite their injuries being medically incompatible with that level of recovery. The brain's potential is remarkable, and continues to amaze researchers with its capacity to adapt, recover and develop new abilities that are not explainable within our

How Can You Harness The Power Of The Mind?

current level of understanding. So please don't limit your expectations!

All living beings have energy associated with them, and it is believed that thoughts also have energy that creates positive or negative effects. Respecting the fact that even thoughts can create real outcomes reinforces the need to make sure that your thoughts are positive and NITs are avoided. It is wrong to think that "it is only a thought inside my head and therefore has no effects on anyone or anything," as all your thoughts affect yourself and others in ways far greater than ever imagined.

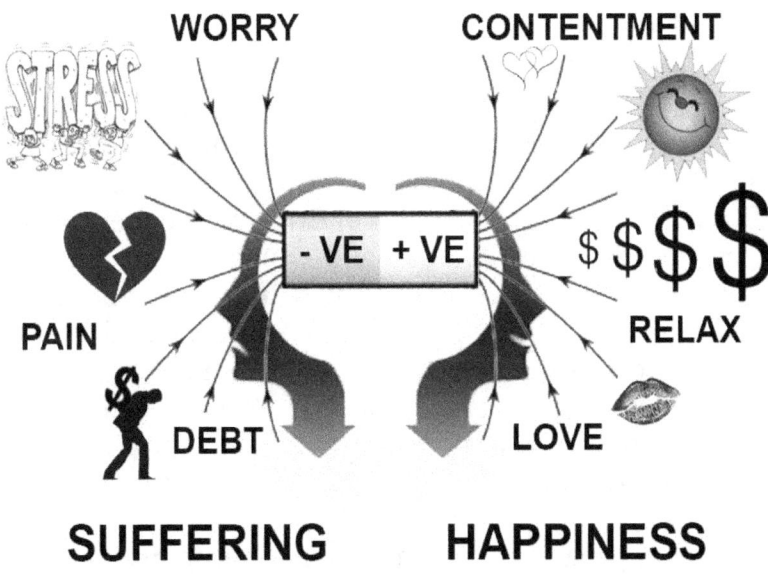

Diagram 1.   The magnetic effect of positive and negative thoughts

The mind can be compared to a massive magnet, with our thoughts having the ability to draw to us the things that we focus on, think about and that we believe to be true. Over time, therefore, our external world progressively mirrors and matches our internal beliefs, thoughts and perceptions.

As a result our mind does a fantastic job in attracting people, events and situations to confirm our beliefs! This fundamental principle exists, and whether we like it or not is irrelevant, as either way your thoughts will affect your future. This reinforces the importance of eliminating NITs from your conscious and subconscious mind. Eliminating NITs will result in better outcomes in your life.

Imagine this. Your day commences with something relatively small going wrong, leaving you annoyed and with a bad attitude. Instantly you create the expectation that you are going to have a bad day. Your scowling face would not cheer up anyone around you and just like a domino effect, something else will go wrong. This then confirms your belief that you are going to have a terrible day and worsens your attitude even more. The downward spiral intensifies, and you even miss seeing the great stuff that is happening around you as you are only focused on the disasters. You are continually finding evidence to support your initial NIT as you affirm to yourself, and everyone around you, that your day is going from bad to worse and no surprises… it does!

A better approach would have been to recognise the NITs after the first event, reverse and control that one thought. Then you can start focusing on having a great day and successfully and happily fixing up any problems facing you. As you are such a "skilled and successful person", you are easily able to handle every event thrown at you. This is the Universal Law of Attraction at its best, just confirming your beliefs and creating what you are focusing on. The important point of this, though, is knowing that it works so you can focus on the positive and reap the rewards instead of attracting more negative events in your life. When you start focusing on the really great stuff that you want to draw into your life, amazing things do happen.

It is considered that we live in an "intelligent universe" that responds with mirroring and matching our thoughts and our beliefs. Through this process your mind will find a way of attracting to you all the things you spend time thinking about. Successful, happy people draw to them more success, as this is what they are expecting will happen. The same goes for unhappy, unsuccessful folk. They expect not to get any breaks in life, not to get a promotion, not to get the partner of their dreams, and continue to live with a negative attitude and often put other people's success down to "just luck".

Sylvia

Elizabeth: Sylvia's story might sound familiar to you. Sometime ago Sylvia phoned me to ask my opinion about a job she was thinking of applying for as a phlebotomist. She had no previous experience taking blood or working in pathology, but wanted to get out of the job she was doing. She needed some convincing, as her doubtfulness was also due to the fact that she was over fifty.

After convincing her that her maturity and life experience gave her a significant advantage, I suggested that the company would be crazy not to employ her. Plus she was a compassionate person who had many great attributes; she was armed with a positive attitude and was definitely confident enough to go to the interview.

I offered to continue to support her efforts on the condition that she remain positive and not let a single NIT destroy her belief in herself, even though many people had applied for the position and had more experience than her in the field. I kept on telling her she would get the position and to make the appropriate plans for the shift in the near future. Casting all doubts aside, she followed my instructions and believed the job was hers and guess what? She was right!

Can we recommend that you approach job interviews positively thinking about what benefits you can bring to the position that others don't have, along with the benefits of your specific skills or life experiences. Again, your mind will do the best job it can in attracting the outcome you think about and focus on, especially if strong positive emotion is attached. This whole attitude flip-changes the feeling of the interview and changes the reception you will get from the interviewers. You will come across as the sort of person they want in their business, as you are positive, cheerful, happy, accommodating and again, the Law of Attraction kicks in and you attract what you focus on.

The Dalai Lama experience

Elizabeth: Another favourite and magical example of the Law of Attraction occurred a few years ago., A female doctor friend and I went to Brisbane, 1000km away from our home in Mackay, for training, only to find that the Dalai Lama – a favourite speaker of mine – was going to be there and speaking at the Entertainment Centre the very same night. I was elated; as I had wanted to see him speak for many years, but soon found that tickets had sold out several months prior to the event.

"How can I be so close, yet so far?" I thought, as the Dalai Lama's busy schedule was restricting him from travelling outside of India as much, and now he was right here in the same city as me. Coincidence or destiny? I phoned John and told him I was definitely going to find a way to see His Holiness speak, and not only that, but I was going to be sitting right in front of him to soak up his greatness! I kept on affirming, everywhere I went, my plan to see His Holiness and it was met with NITs left, right and centre. "You'll never get in," "No tickets available for months," "You'll not get through the front gate without a ticket because of major security," etc. Basically no one believed in me.

Under my instruction, my friend made a promise to me that if she was to accompany me to hear him speak, then she would have to follow my instructions and believe, as I did, that we would see him without a doubt or a negative thought. She was a little concerned, as she was not as skilled as I was in this regard, and after teaching her a few key NIT protectors, she eagerly agreed to the adventure.

We had meetings all that day, and every person that asked me what our plans were that night, I replied that we were seeing the Dalai Lama. "What, with no tickets?" was the reply. "You won't get in…" – NITs, NITs, NITs, but I was passionate and most of all positive. "I will see the Dalai Lama," I told them with gusto.

The last appointment finished at 4.30pm, and as planned it was close to the Entertainment Centre. The sales rep asked if she could drive us somewhere as she had picked us up for the meeting at her office. So I replied "Yes, to the Entertainment Centre please!" She laughed, as she knew our plight, but agreed to take us; she herself had tried in vain to purchase tickets a month earlier. We were a few minutes late, and everyone had moved inside except the armed guards, which made my friend twitchy and nervous.

Officials and security guards with stern faces were posted at each set of boom gates that we approached, and to our driver's amazement, we were allowed through without being asked for tickets! We slowly made our way one by one through each barrier, and the boom gates were lifted allowing us to pass through with no questions asked. Our driver dropped us as close to the front of the Entertainment Centre entrance as cars were permitted. With an "I don't know how you've made it this far," expression written all over her face, she drove away smiling and shaking her head in disbelief.

"What now?" said my friend. Looking bewildered, with no one around except the stiff guards gathered around talking about twenty metres away from us, I said "We go there!" I pointed to the guards and instructed my friend not to say anything. I told her that I would do the talking and to just follow me. At this point I still didn't have a plan, only a mission.

Mastering Negative Impulsive Thoughts (NITs)

We approached a particularly serious official-looking gentleman. Towering over us, he asked, "Can I help you?"

I replied, "I believe you have tickets."

"What name?" he asked as he searched through the envelopes.

"Nope... no... no names like that here."

I was pleased about that, as I was not about to compromise my values and take someone else's tickets, so I said, "That's strange; I believed you had my tickets." I followed this up with, "Do you have any other tickets without names on them?"

"Only these two with nothing on them," he said, and paused as he loosely waved them in front of me.

"Well, they must be for us then!" I said, and gently eased them from his loose grasp and headed rapidly for the entrance.

My friend's eyes were as big as saucers and she could not speak a word as we were ushered to our seats by the door attendant. Our seats were ten rows from the front, right in the middle and there was His Holiness just as I imagined him, right in front of us in what I would describe as one of the best seats in the house!

This story illustrates the power of controlling and banishing any NITs that would keep me from my goal. My own steadfastly positive mind set and determination not to give up helped me believe that I would sit in the presence of His Holiness. Even though it was a long shot, the odds were stacked against me, and no-one believed it was possible except me, my friend and my beautiful husband the ever-positive John. Guess what? I was right!

As we delve deeper into this phenomenon, it gets more and more interesting. There is another key ingredient that tends to occur naturally and turns ordinary thoughts into powerhouse thoughts that magnify the effects. This is the presence of strong emotion. That's right, the more emotion behind the thought, the more powerful it becomes, and this works for both positive and negative thoughts.

> Thus, NITs linked to strong emotion will have a magnified negative effect, just like positive thoughts linked to strong emotion will have a greater positive effect. This just reinforces the need to eliminate NITs, but I think we have said that before once or twice! Is the message getting through? Is it clear yet?

The Physiology of Feeling Great

The strong relationship between the thoughts that you think and the way you feel is reasonably obvious, but it is much more profound than most people know. There are many excellent studies that prove what you think is much more powerful than your actual reality. For example, the brain is unable to differentiate an experience that is imagined from one that is actually experienced. Exactly the same feel-good chemicals called endorphins and encephalins are released, the same feel-good centres like the amygdala are activated, and the person gets the same feeling of euphoria in both situations. This has been confirmed under controlled trials using MRI scanners to detect the activity of the brain centres.

It has also been shown by artificially creating "happy actions" in the absence of "happy events" that the same feel-good hormones and centres are activated. Laughing yoga is a good example of this, and the act of laughing and smiling itself sets off euphoric feelings in the brain.

Clearly the opposite is also true, with NITs causing negative feelings, and even negative posture contributes to feeling bad. So just imagining bad events will have the same effect on your body as if you were actually living through them. This is a very good reason for controlling your NITs! Other examples are watching movies or TV programs that are full of violence or negativity. Coming out of those experiences, you feel washed out, exhausted, and drained of energy as if you have been through the whole trauma yourself – well, emotionally you have! Your mind has experienced it as if it is you that has been through that whole devastating process. If the film or program is overwhelmingly negative, you are going to have work extra hard to lift yourself out of the deep hole of negativity and get some positive good thoughts in there to negate all of that bad energy.

Controlling your exposure to NITs, from any source, is therefore important and while the NITs from certain films are obvious and immediate, the NITs from other sources are just as damaging whether they are from your workmates, friends, enemies, competitive businesses or the media. The feelings that you experience are real and are taken on board as your reality. The experiences are felt as if it was you personally going through the whole thing – whether it is a film or false denigration from others. So choose well what experiences you expose your emotions to and what energy you allow to affect your personal space.

An extreme example of media negativity leading to a catastrophic outcome would be the newspaper description of singer/song writer Karen Carpenter as being a "chubby girl". This throwaway comment led to the downwards spiral of her self-image to the point of anorexia and ultimately her early death.

On the flip side, fortunately by imagining all the wonderful things happening that you desire and watching feel-good movies and programs, you can cause the release of all the great emotional responses and internal changes to make you feel great even before the outcomes have materialised. The feeling is worth it, knowing that you are on track to reap the rewards of the positive approach whilst enjoying the journey.

The Physical Brain Changes from NITs

The relationship between the mind and the body is far from understood, and the power of the mind is far greater than we currently know. It is known that we only use about 10% of our brain capacity, and many incredible things have been proven to occur that clearly show how we underestimate what we can achieve. So from the start, we need to avoid putting limitations on our expectations.

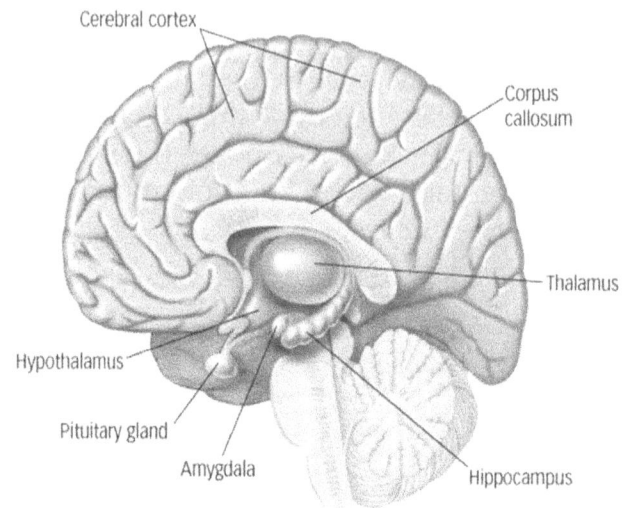

The role of the Amygdala

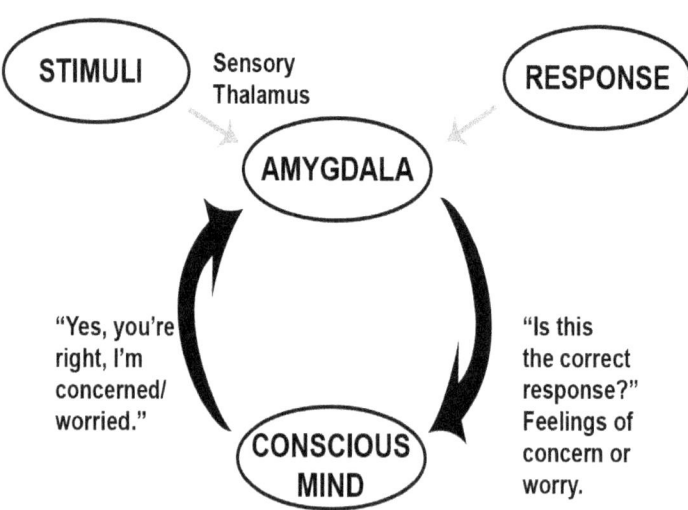

Diagram 2.   Role of the Amygdala in responses

How Can You Harness The Power Of The Mind?

Positive thoughts and good posture release the feel-good hormones and activate the amygdala. This activates your immune system and makes your resistance to infection and body systems work better. There are documented cases of self-healing using just the power of the mind, and Eastern gurus and religious leaders across faiths* have been shown to perform fantastic feats of regeneration of body parts.

This astonishing power of the mind also has a flip side where negative forces can cause physical and mental suffering and actual disease.

HEALTH WARNING

Negative Thinking causes :

- 9 years reduced life span
- Significantly more stokes
- 43% more heart attacks
- 50% more deaths from heart disease
- Increased risk of cancer
- Reduced quality of life
- Increased depression and anxiety
- Increased infections
- Measurable falls in anti-oxidant levels

Here is a small sample of the evidence. Research from the USA showed that strokes increase by 9% for every step toward negativity that people have in a 16-point negativity scale (Ann Arbor, July 21, 2011 *Stroke*).

---

* Jesus in the Bible regenerated the ear of a man that had just had it cut off. Various other saints, wise people and gurus have been recorded as performing healing "miracles" around the world, in all cultures, beliefs and religions. Also see examples in Autobiography of a Yogi by Paramahansa Yogananda.

This was after removing other variables and risk factors, and these significant increases in stroke from the research were shown to be directly from negative thinking.

A study from Holland revealed that there were significantly fewer heart attacks in the people with a positive outlook on life, again adjusted for other risk factors (February 26, 2006 Archives of Internal Medicine). The extent of the difference is astounding, with the drop being 43% less in the most optimistic group! These results were duplicated in a study showing a 50% reduced death rate from heart disease in optimistic people (Steptoe et al, Br J Health *Psychol* 2006:11(1).

Similarly, stress and negative emotional experiences as a child lead to 30-70% more heart disease as an adult after removal of other risk factors (Dong et al, September 20, 2004 *Circulation*).

Danner et al published in Nature in 2001, a study of 180 nuns that showed that those with a positive and optimistic outlook in their twenties resulted in a nine-year increased life expectancy. This was a quality research study because it removed other variables within the group of nuns living in such a controlled environment with identical lifestyles. It therefore gives very powerful evidence that it was the positive emotional state of those nuns that led to the extra nine years of life!

There are many studies that show that optimism heavily influences mental and physical illnesses as well as quality of life outcomes (Conversano et al, *Clinical Practice and Epidemiology in Mental Illness*, May 2010).

On a much simpler note, but equally astounding, is that studies have shown that positive thinking is also known to have increased resistance to the common cold. Measurable increases in anti-oxidant levels were found in optimistic people (Boehm et al, *Psychosomatic Medicine*, Jan 2013) and this is clearly one of the reasons that optimistic thinkers will have the wide range of health benefits as previously stated.

Repeated research also reveals the powerful effect of the mind with between 60-74% of physical symptoms being caused by the mind, with no organic pathology (Textbook *Primary Care Mental Health*, edited Linda Gask). Also 50-71% of presentations to family doctors are psychosomatic, otherwise known as "somatoform" symptoms (Fink et al, *Psychosomatics* 1999 Vol 40, issue 4) with no physical basis for the symptoms.

The surprising thing about all of these studies is not only that the differences exist, but the dramatic increase in symptoms, illnesses and death resulting from having a negative emotional state or attitude. It confirms the power of thoughts as having energy and a major influence on your health and well-being, even in the absence of those thoughts being spoken.

> It is therefore indisputable that negative attitudes, thoughts and experiences lead to increased illnesses of many types and a shorter life. As we quoted from Chapter 1: "Watch your thoughts… they become your destiny"!

For a bit of fun, we would ask you to try a couple of simple experiments that show how you can artificially boost your attitude and mood, as your body's posture and physical attitude will be mirrored in your emotional state.

Mastering Negative Impulsive Thoughts (NITs)

Diagram 3.   Ecstasy Position

Experiment 1

Hold yourself in the "ecstasy position" above, with your back arched and your head back, your arms elevated and stretched behind you, looking up at the sky, and hold a really big smile. Breathe deeply and slowly and hold that position for three minutes only. When you are finished, how do you feel? Amazing, isn't it? Nothing has changed, but you feel happier!

Experiment 2

Adopt the same posture as above, this time while grinning as hard as you can and looking upward. Try to think of something depressing, and although you may be able to think of a topic, it is amazingly difficult to feel depressed while holding this position.

So the three lessons from this chapter include:

- Having a happy posture and laughing will create a euphoric feeling in the absence of a happy reality.
- Imagining your positive future will give you exactly the same euphoria as actually having it.

- You will live longer and have fewer illnesses by having a positive outlook.

The old adage of "fake it until you make it!" does have some value here, as faking a positive outlook will make you feel better and you will become more positive over time. Of course, we still need to teach you the steps to eliminate and treat NITs when you do come across them, but you are now well skilled at recognising them. Together with this background information about how the brain works and the power of your thoughts, your understanding of the importance of living a NIT-free life should be strong and give you the desire to develop a NIT-free zone and live a wonderfully happy NIT-free life!

Summary

Every one of us can use the physiological laws of the mind and body and the Laws of Attraction for our own benefit. We just need to understand how they work and how to harness that power. Focus on the wonderful things in life and experiences of wonderful things will happen to you! (If you focus on the opposite, the opposite will happen too, so make sure you don't focus on negative things!)

"Fake it until you make it" to get the beneficial physiological responses in your mind and body working for your benefit, even while you imagine the success that you are working towards. Research and MRI studies confirm that positive thinking does make you live longer, reduce heart attacks and strokes, actively fight infections and makes you feel better.

Take advantage of the power of the mind and start harnessing the universal Laws of Attraction and to create your universe as you wish it to be while enjoying the journey along the way!

5
How Do You Treat Your Own Negative Impulsive Thoughts?

> "The more you depend on forces outside yourself, the more you are dominated by them."
> **Harold Sherman**

First take responsibility and stop blaming others

The first step towards any success in life is to take full responsibility for where you are now and where you are going. This principle is well established and described in many books, including Napoleon Hill's book from 1937 *Think and Grow Rich*, the more recent book by Stephen Covey, *7 Habits of Highly Successful People*, and Jack Canfield's, *The Success Principles*. It is not a new principle; it has stood the test of time and continues to be the cornerstone to taking control of your own life and determining your future success and happiness.

Who is driving your bus? Who is in control of your life? Do you take responsibility for absolutely everything in your life, where you are and why you are there?

Where are you now? Think about all the choices and actions that have occurred to get you to this point. Obviously things have happened either because of things you have done, or perhaps things you have not done. Either way, the choice has been yours, and your actions or inactions have resulted in you being exactly where you are at this point.

Of course we hear the howls of protests from some of you who want to think that some of the things in life were not in your control – it was the "fault" of your work, your boss, your spouse, or the economy. You may say "I had no control" over these events... but did you? Was the abusive husband who controlled your life completely out of your control? Was the harassing boss who made your life miserable outside of your control? If you blame the poor economy on your poor personal finances, then why aren't everyone's finances ruined during the years of a bad economy? Are all these things completely out of your control, or was it your choice to accept the situation and not stand up for yourself and change the circumstances? Was it your decision not to call the police or walk out of the abusive situation? Was it your choice not to report the harassment at work? Was it your choice to give those people or the external factors, like the economy, the power over you to affect your happiness, well-being or financial situation? Obviously it was!

This is a really hard pill to swallow, and we know this personally, as both of us have suffered in various situations over the years. Even though the pain and suffering that we experienced was being created by someone close to us, it was our choice to remain in that situation. We kept trying to make it better, trying to help the other party and trying to heal the wounds of everyone that was getting hurt in the collateral damage.

There's an old story about a dog on a farm verandah that howls all day, and when the old farmer in the rocking chair alongside was asked why the dog was howling, he said "He is sitting on a nail". When asked "Well, why doesn't he get off the nail?" The owner just spat his tobacco and said "It hurts enough to howl, but not enough to move away!" Can you identify with the howling dog? Were you only hurt enough to howl but not enough to move away?

We therefore do know how hard it is to accept that we are each personally responsible for where we are and *everything*

How Do You Treat Your Own Negative Impulsive Thoughts?

we have been through. Plus we know how big the mind switch needs to be. It is very likely to create several "Oh my God" moments as you reflect through past events:

- OMG, why did it take me so long to draw the line?
- OMG, why did it take so long to leave?
- OMG, why did I not fight back?
- OMG, why did I not say something?

Please don't despair, because this is the start of your own personal empowerment. For now just look at things and don't judge them at all. You do need to stop putting the blame on external parties or events and start taking full responsibility for your life from now on. That is, from now on! You will start to see things from a different perspective and astounding things will start to happen in your life, as they did in ours.

The truth is that you are completely responsible for your own life and thoughts, and where you are now. Is it where you want to be? Are you on track for where you want to be in the future? This is a huge topic by itself and what we are dealing with in this book is NITs and controlling them. All of the thoughts that are generated in your head are clearly and obviously not anyone else's fault. They are not your partner's fault, your parents' fault or your boss's fault. They are solely being generated by you.

> Take a step back and recognise that everything coming out of your head in the form of your thoughts is well and truly only *your* responsibility. Other people may create challenging situations, cause stress or difficulties around you, or have implanted negative self-defeating ideas in your head throughout your life. But how you handle them and how you let them affect you, is all within your control and is your choice!

Even when terrible events (e.g. natural disasters) occur that are truly not in your control, how you let those events affect you is still in your control. The important thing in that situation is to keep clarity and focus on how you let the events affect you while you support or help the people that need the help. Grieve for, or with, the people who have suffered, and always keep in mind that from our narrow perspective, the greater good is not always obvious!

The great news is that by taking responsibility for where you are right now, it gives you the power to get to where you want to be in the future! Your thoughts really do create your life and they are truly within your control.

A good (and bad) example of failing to take responsibility was seen in a marriage separation in our extended family. Unfortunately, this story has a common theme in today's world. Charleen and Paul married in their early twenties and lived together for twenty years. During this time they had children and ran a construction business together. Charleen was very controlling and didn't ever listen to Paul's advice even though it was his field of expertise. This led to the collapse of the business, and he eventually went out and got retraining and employment elsewhere.

Throughout the marriage, she did not allow him to enjoy his dreams of surfing, travelling and enjoying life, and she was very restrictive with her personal affection and love. She would only do the things that she wanted to do, and even refused to attend the funeral of Paul's father as well as many other family events over the years. The excuse she gave was that "I just don't like funerals!" – But no-one likes funerals. You turn up out of respect for the person and their family!

In the absence of love and affection in the marriage, aggravated by being in an environment of unbalanced power and lack of consideration or respect, eventually the easy-going and flexible Paul had suffered enough and left the marriage. Not really surprising, except for the fact that it took twenty whole years to get to that point.

Of course, the vitriol and abuse that followed towards Paul and the rest of his supportive, loving and affectionate family, was an eye-opening experience. Plus Paul's loving and adoring new partner became the "cause" of all the problems! If you ever need a situation of a NIT-filled environment, this is probably one of the most prolific. Charleen chose not to acknowledge that her actions over the past twenty years had driven Paul into the arms of someone who would provide him with the love and affection that he had been deprived of over all those years. Her failed marriage, failed financial investments, relatively poor financial status, complete exclusion from Paul's family and the failure to mend the marriage was 100% her responsibility because it was caused by her decisions and actions over the years. Unfortunately, this possibility has never seemed to come into her consciousness, as she continues to blame everyone else, including the family, for "keeping Paul from me". Until she takes responsibility, she will be trapped and unable to take full control of her life and any chance of future happiness.

The flip side is also that Paul is 100% responsible for being in that situation for twenty years! He allowed Charleen to rule the roost and control his everyday activities. He allowed her to kill his passions and dreams, not act on his better financial judgment and not have an affectionate and loving relationship. He did not communicate effectively how important it was for him to be loved or the importance of family events like his father's funeral. Now, by finally taking responsibility for his own life and making his own decisions about the way he wants to live his own life, he is happier, healthier and on track for his own success.

> So, no matter what side of the fence you are on, you are fully responsible for where you are now, either by making it happen or by allowing it to be done to you. It can be a very bitter pill to swallow, especially when situations get unpleasant, but the 100% responsibility rule still holds true.

Mastering Negative Impulsive Thoughts (NITs)

Matt Changes the Course of History!

We have another great story, about a man called Matt, whose success story is that of the classic overweight, down-and-out person who finally takes responsibility and pulls himself out of the pit of bad habits by choosing a different life path. This transformation is achievable by anyone, and only takes a decision and then persistence and dedication.

As health professionals, we are often faced with a patient who claims that "I hardly eat anything, exercise well, but am still unable to lose weight. My mother is the same, so I believe it is my metabolism that stops me from losing weight!" Where is the responsibility here? Out of the patient's hands and completely controlled by the dreaded metabolism, so with that great excuse the patient is really telling us that they will never succeed in losing weight, so what is the point in trying. Their unspoken attitude is "Definitely don't make me work hard to lose this weight or change my favourite foods of pies, chips, pizzas and high-calorie fizzy drinks!"

Matt, on the other hand, was in a family that went through a traumatic marital separation when he was ten years old. He was very upset through that time, to the point that he missed a lot of his school years. He also ate progressively more unhealthy foods as the parental direction was aimed at making him feel good (rather than be good), and no priority was placed on getting good grades. His weight increased steadily throughout his school years, as his habits of fish, chips, burgers and pizzas, washed down with the usual canned soft drinks, took their inevitable toll. His habit of staying up through the night to play online war games worsened, and his physical activity levels fell. He slept more through the day and stayed up more through the night, very seldom getting out in the day or participating in any social activities.

Without any reasonable school grades, Matt could only get low-level jobs labouring or as a shop assistant, with the associated

How Do You Treat Your Own Negative Impulsive Thoughts?

low-level pay and conditions. He was also embarrassed by his weight and appearance, which had the effect of reducing him to playing computer games and avoiding social activities and events. This had the additional negative effect of a limited social life and deterioration of his self-esteem, and definitely lessened or eliminated the possibility of getting girlfriends!

By the age of twenty, he was 110kg at 176cm, giving him a BMI (body mass index)* of 35.5, where normal is 20-25, overweight is 25-30, obese is 30-35 and >35 is morbidly obese. This means that Matt's weight level could have morbid (damaging/dangerous) effects on his health. This situation is unfortunately now becoming more and more common, as habits like Matt's are becoming more accepted behaviour in the developed world.

To get out of this downward spiral of bad habits, each person has to make a single decision to change. Matt's motivation came from within – from acknowledging that his life was not going anywhere and that he was not where he wanted to be. He could also see that he was not taking steps to get where he wanted to be in the future.

He made the decision to take responsibility for his own life and stop blaming his parents, his metabolism, his anxiety, his poor school results, etc. He set himself two simple goals:

- To get his weight down to 70kg.
- To get into university and get an IT degree.

In his own mind, he took responsibility for his future and did not rely on anyone else or put any blame outside himself as he worked out how to get out of the hole he was in.

---

* To calculate your own BMI, get your height in metres and your weight in Kgs and divide your weight by your height squared (Wt / Height x Height)

Matt's computer skills stood him in good stead, as he investigated both weight loss and university requirements online. He started to reduce the obvious excess calorie intake by cutting out fizzy drinks, and started to do some active walking to burn off calories. Within a short time, some success was evident, with his weight falling. He used this success as proof that he could succeed, and progressively improved his food intake and exercise levels to bring about more positive change. It was not easy, as the weight did not come off smoothly – there were times when he would lose weight and then it would sit there, not changing for weeks at a time. With professional guidance and using online information, he was able to modify what he was doing and he progressively saw the kilograms fall off.

The wonderful thing, even before his weight was decreasing, was that after starting to eat better foods and beginning the exercise process, he felt more energetic, alert, enthusiastic and great in himself! The medical explanation for this is that a better diet alone will improve the way you feel, and the higher exercise levels release the encephalins and endorphins that are your feel-good hormones. So even before the weight-loss benefits kick in, you are feeling much better in yourself.

The next step for him was to get a final-year school grade, and despite being a few years out of school, he enrolled in a program to do his final school year again. Though this time he put his head down and worked diligently to get the grades he needed. The real-life implications of working with no qualifications were now a reality to him, so he had the motivation to do the "boring" stuff and get the good grades. A year later he finished his final school grades, at the age of twenty, got the grades he needed, and was accepted to study an IT degree in the capital.

The following year, he made the trip from his rural home town to the state capital, very scared and insecure. He'd never been out of town, and still had never really socialised because of the obesity stigma among his friends. Now as a 70kg, healthy, fit and trim, mature first-year student and with personal successes under his now narrower belt, he became a very popular leader that many looked up to due to his life experience and independence. Very quickly he developed a large group of friends, found himself a serious girlfriend and has continued to succeed at his university course. As well as keeping up his sensible eating and exercise routine, enjoying his wonderful new relationship and planning for a successful and happy future.

Compare this to the insecure, obese, unhealthy person who two years earlier had no future, the likelihood of social isolation, medical illnesses, poor quality of life and an early death. What Matt has achieved here can be achieved by anyone – it just takes a single decision, full responsibility and following through with the actions. As the saying goes:

"At any moment you can choose to change your life, but what moment will you choose?"

In relation to NITs, clearly the NITs that come out of you can only be controlled by you, and the thoughts in this situation would need to be along the lines of:

"I am on track to get to my target weight. Just keep on going. I love the extra energy that the exercise is giving me. I love the way I feel so much more alert because I am eating good, natural and nutritious foods. I am choosing the healthy foods to help me on the path to success. I deserve to succeed".

The NITs that clearly need to be rapidly obliterated are often along the lines of "I will never lose the weight. I failed before so I will fail again. Oh, what's the point in trying? Just one donut will not matter. Exercise is such a pain. I hate doing this…"

Make the decision, take the action, control the NITs and enjoy the success!

Create a positive feeling when performing positive actions

When performing activities that are healthy and beneficial like exercise or healthy eating, it is critical that your thoughts and feelings during those times need to be positive, otherwise your body will react to that negative feeling and create problems like injuries, strains or pains to "protect" you from this negative experience.

A good exercise it to look at people who are running along the side of the road and try to see if they are enjoying it or hating it. Body posture and facial expression usually make it very obvious, and the ones who are thinking "This is great; this exercise is doing me good and will get me stronger/lighter/in better shape/more energy" will have great posture, more bounce and vitality, as the positive energy empowers the whole body.

The people who are doing the activity with predominant NITs in their head like "I hate exercise, what a pain this is, I will never be able to do this, that stupid doctor..." are very likely to have poor posture and look like they are suffering. They are unlikely to sustain the exercise long-term and are more likely to have injuries or physical problems. Your logical brain knows that the thing you are doing is going to be good for you, so it is important to create the good feelings in your body to match those positive effects.

So even if you don't feel like you have the energy before you start, have to drag yourself out of bed the extra thirty minutes earlier or have already done a twelve-hour shift of physically tiring work, eliminate all those NITs. Replace them with the thoughts of "I will have so much more energy after I have done this run. The stress of the day will be gone after I have finished this exercise. I will be able to solve all the problems more easily after I have done this activity!" And you will – trust me, I'm a doctor! (Always wanted to say that but it is not usually appropriate…)

"Can I really control my own thoughts?"

A lot of people will react to the concept of NITs by claiming that they have no control over their thoughts and that a situation automatically makes them feel a certain way or react in a certain way. The concept is shown in the diagram (4a), where external events that are experienced by the person result in the reaction. Obviously, this reaction is different for different people, with each of us processing the same information and coming up with a different reaction. However, because the learned reaction for each person has been so established over many years, the person then believes that it is automatic and "beyond their control".

This is absolutely not the case, as the processing step that occurs in the brain between the event and the reaction is completely within our control, and with active choice we can determine a different reaction to be played out in our thoughts, words and emotions. In this way, the same event will result in the newly chosen and designed reaction, with different and better emotional and practical outcomes. (Diagram 4b)

Mastering Negative Impulsive Thoughts (NITs)

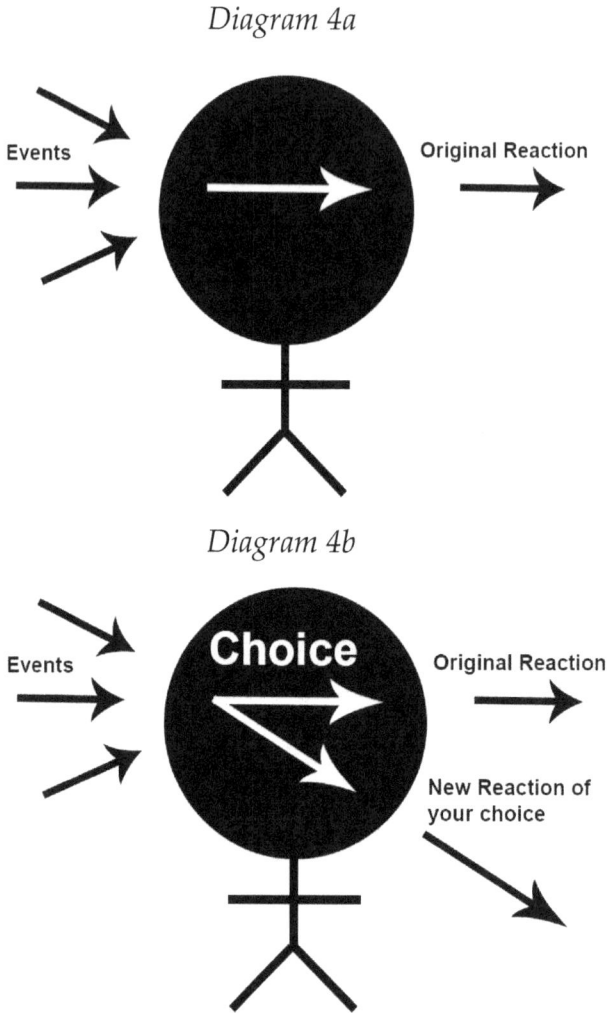

Diagram 4a

Diagram 4b

Reactions are in your control

The key to taking control of your emotions in any recurring situation is to actively choose your preferred response, with your thought processes and your attached emotions clearly chosen. You can then rehearse that behaviour over and over in

How Do You Treat Your Own Negative Impulsive Thoughts?

your mind, so that you have the pattern established. This is very much like having a video recording playing out a particular scene, with you as the director in control and not the victim just reacting to the events. (Your dialogue may include I will not overreact, I will listen carefully and then respond calmly). Next, you have to put the scene into action with the event, and for the first few times you will need to force yourself to "act" the part and perform the scene as close to the imagined scene as you can. The more often you do it, the better you become, and the more automatic it will become until eventually this will be your new automatic response, not the old unhelpful reaction.

You will be amazed how well the process works, often with the first attempt. The new behaviour quickly becomes automatic as the new positive results reinforce the advantages of the new response. Everyone wins!

You can then look at other difficult situations that you struggle with and put in place other responses that change the situation from a difficult one into a reasonable one. One example of this would be the conflict that arises when a drug-seeking patient is requesting from a doctor something that is medically unwarranted, like an inappropriate narcotic or addictive medication.

Doctors are trained over many years to work with patients and try to fix their problems, but are suddenly in a situation with conflict between the request from the patient and appropriate medicine and what would be best for the patient. The drug-seeker tells extremely convincing stories as to why the drugs were lost, stolen, prescription destroyed in the wash, or they're going travelling abroad so need extra medications, etc. In the event of the medication not being provided, the response from the patient will often be hostile or violent, which adds potential fear to the volatile situation.

The thought processes for the doctor would often be the automatic sinking feeling of "Oh my goodness, this will be another struggle", because their reaction arises from their previous experiences of struggling to get the patient to understand and agree to their position and the typically hostile end result. The alternative pathway that results in no stress for the doctor is to have a pre-determined plan and emotional outcome of peace and tranquility. This is achieved by using a set of conditions and rules that must be adhered to for the medications to be supplied in whatever medically appropriate conditions that doctor has set. Very early on in the consultation, the conditions are made clear to the patient, one of which is that any raised voice, violence, aggression or breach of the "rules" will result in the relationship being terminated immediately.

This is an example of the doctor controlling the reactions of the other person as well as their own, resulting in a much better outcome for the patient as well the doctor, as they then know that the manipulative behaviour of threatening violence will not work.

Another example of planning your response is in the situation with your challenging teenage children, where they are being abusive and insulting. In the past the typical reaction may have been to get angry and shout back. The much better response of calmness and non-responsiveness is set out in the section dealing with children (chapter 8). You maintain your dignity and class, and you deal with the problem at hand in a way that the children will learn from.

Visualise Yourself as a Positive Person

Visualising yourself as a positive person is a very useful conscious decision to make, as it sets the foundation for everything that your mind produces. Once you have established yourself as a positive person, the nature of your thoughts will follow that predetermined nature so the quantity of NITs will be significantly reduced. This process is a learned behaviour too, so as with all habits, visualise yourself as a positive person, behaving in that way even if you have to "fake it until you make it".

If you do not know how to handle a particular situation that you are being faced with, imagine what your most respected positive thinker would say or do when faced with that same situation. Then act, think and feel in the way that this mentor would behave. Obviously it will be much easier once you have got the strategies in place to eliminate and replace the NITs, so that is the next step.

Replacing NITs

Like any other habit, the NITs habit can be broken and replaced with much more productive forms of thinking, and like any other behaviour that one wishes to change, one must start firstly with a plan. There are many strategies to choose from and we recommend you try each one as an exercise to work out which technique suits you the best. Clearly each one of us is unique and different, and how we learn new ways and establish new habits will vary greatly from person to person, so interestingly what works for you may not be effective for the next person.

Elaborating on this a little more will give you a greater understanding of yourself and give you tricks that can fast-track your learning. Everyone processes information in certain ways and these are mainly visual, auditory and kinesthetic – in other words seeing, hearing or feeling. Whichever of these areas you naturally use will be the most effective process for you to use in breaking the NIT habit. You will be able to use your visual processes to destroy the NITs if you are visual, use sound strategies if you are auditory and emotional strategies if you are kinesthetic.

VISUAL

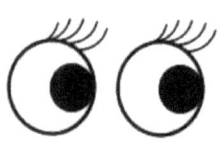

Let me see it
I see what you mean
That looks fine
The future looks bright
Show me what you mean
Lets look at it from a different perspective

OR

AUDITORY

That sounds great
Listen here
I hear what you're saying
I like to sound things out
I like the sound of that

OR

KINESTHETIC

That feels right to me
I'll just get my head around it
Get a grip on yourself
You're all heart
She's so prickly
I get a good feeling about that

Diagram 5. Visual, Auditory and Kinesthetic processing

So how do you know where you fall in these categories? Everyone has a basic idea of how they learn the best. Some people can clearly visualise what someone is saying and see it in their minds. They will also tend to make comments like "I see what you mean", "I get the picture" or "Look here." Their preference will be to see pictures, DVDs or view the details on paper so they can understand the issue fully. This is also the most common way of operating.

Auditory people will learn best with sounds, speech, and music, and they will prefer to have the details explained to them directly. Their comments will tend to be "I hear what you are saying," "Sounds like a good idea" or "That rings a bell." They will prefer to listen to a presentation rather than read the papers on the subject in front of them.

Kinesthetic people are the emotional ones, who respond best to "feel and touch" in both emotional and physical ways. So if you are in this group, you would use expressions like "I feel good about this," "I have a hunch that this will work," "I am afraid you are right/wrong" or "This is a rock solid proposal." If you are in this group, you will learn best by being actively involved in the process, getting your hands dirty and physically doing it yourself. Best results will be achieved when you are emotionally involved or "sold" on the principle. This is because of your ability to relate emotionally to benefits of the issue which may be for you personally or for other people around you or in the broader community. You like to get physically involved and do the things, touch the products and be involved emotionally.

People commonly have a blend of these types, so you may able to relate to more than one category. However understanding how you learn best will help in selecting the best strategies for you in dealing with NITs and in your broader life processes. It is also a very important skill when dealing with other people because using the correct communication process will have dramatic effects on getting your message across.

Can you identify what category you fall into and do you function predominantly in one or more than one category? You can use the following NIT-busting strategies to test which of the strategies works best for you, and that will also give you a clearer idea of your predominant processing modality.

NIT-Buster for Visual Processors: Stop, Drop and Roll

Firstly recognise the NIT and confirm its nature with the three questions:

- Is it proven to be the truth?
- Is it positive, empowering and uplifting to all?
- Is it taking me towards my goals?

We will now take you through the nice and simple three-step Stop, Drop and Roll process that will allow you to remove the NITs.

Let us assume you have just recognised a NIT within your thought processes, like "I am stupid and I will never get this right!" In a work situation, you may have been shown a new task and you are now doing it by yourself for the first time and have just done it incorrectly. That NIT pops up in your head, and now that you are aware of its presence, you need to take immediate and decisive action! As a visual person, you could imagine seeing flashing lights go off in your brain as you become aware of the alarm for NITs. You can see these words scrolling across your mind: "I AM STUPID AND I WILL NEVER GET THIS RIGHT!"

- **STOP.** First you need to stop the NIT. Take action immediately by freezing the letters or stop them in their tracks. They need to be stopped, frozen, contained or quarantined, just like any contagious disease. See the letters being frozen with ice or throw a net over them – whatever way is best for

How Do You Treat Your Own Negative Impulsive Thoughts?

you. Your aim is that the NIT you can see is stopped, unable to escape and is contained for you to go to the next step, which will be to destroy it.

- **DROP**. This is the removal process. In your head you can see the thoughts or words that are trapped and now they need to be eliminated in whatever way you see fit. One of the most popular ways is by visualising PacMan from the computer game, who will march across the letters munching on the negative thoughts. These "Positive PacMen" can seek and destroy NITs whenever you require them to.

- **ROLL**. This is the process of rolling the NIT into the positive alternative. So after the NIT is removed, this space needs to be replaced with a Positive Affirmative Thought (PAT). This is the positive version or exactly the opposite of the NIT that has just been destroyed. In this situation, the comment of "I am stupid and I will never get this right" is immediately replaced with a statement like "I am proud of myself for learning this new task and with a bit more practice will master it." Alternatively, "I am a good learner and every new skill takes practice. Mistakes are part of the learning process so I am getting better with every attempt".

This replacement of the NIT with a PAT needs to be done within seconds, and is a skill that improves with practice. Delay at this point gives the NIT the chance to recover and regain strength. Like any bad habit, you can't leave a vacant space; you have to put a new habit in its place.

Alternative visual effects for the NIT destruction are seeing the NIT being melted down as a puddle and then drying up. You might also see the NIT being dropped into a fire and burned in flames. If you are into computer games, you might also shoot down the NITs with a powerful gun or bazooka and see it explode into pieces. You could also imagine using the delete button on the computer so that when you choose to remove the thoughts, hit delete and the words disappear. Nice and fast, clean and effective, and this option is popular with young tech-savvy generations. If you relate to cleaning, you could use a cleaning agent and just wipe out the letters like words on a dusty car. The options are endless and you need to find the process that works best for you. By practicing the process you will respond faster and it will become more automatic over time.

NIT-Busters for Auditory Processors

A classic auditory processing person crossed our path when we were running a No-NITs training session as part of a health retreat we conducted on the tropical island paradise of Gili Trawangan, between Bali and Lombok. The same group of islands was visited by Elizabeth Gilbert in her book Eat, Pray, Love. This lady in the retreat could not relate to the visual exercises in the NIT destruction as mentioned above, saying "I hear what you are saying, and I can see the NITs in my head, but I can't keep my focus enough to destroy them." Clearly her visual processing was much weaker than her auditory, so we modified the exercise to suit her auditory processing.

The next step was to get her to imagine the words that had just been said in her head as a tape recording and hear the words being rewound backwards with the high-pitched squealing that you get – Woolloomooloo! With the words taken back, she replaced them with the positive alternative and this worked very well for her.

Alternative auditory processes would be to hear the words and imagine turning the sound down to zero so the words become quiet and then disappear. Then, when replaced with the PAT, turn up the volume again so that it is strong and powerful and the NIT has no chance of being heard.

NIT-Busters for Kinesthetic People

A kinesthetic person works with feelings and emotions as their most powerful driver, but they will usually also have visual or auditory abilities. They would then often draw on either the visual or auditory process for the above exercise, so these strategies may be effective. However, for some people who have a very dominant kinesthetic nature, they will respond better creating the feelings and emotions that the NIT presents and changing that feeling to a positive one.

The kinesthetic person will often "take things to heart" and be more "sensitive", using terms like "I was mortified" and "I couldn't believe…", and create emotional responses from passing comments made by others without having meant to have that effect. So when the kinesthetic person thinks about themselves as being "fat," they "feel" fat or unattractive and unlikely to feel attractive to the person of their dreams. To deal with kinesthetic NITs, especially if visual or auditory processes don't work, the feelings and emotions have to be changed.

Firstly recognise the negative emotion that your thoughts have produced and go through the Stop, Drop and Roll process. Stop the emotional NIT immediately by ceasing all emotional reactions to it and take a step back and detach yourself from it. If the feeling is a NIT, a positive emotion needs to replace it. You currently have the thought or emotion stopped or suspended until you think of an appropriate way to Drop it and then Roll it over into a positive emotion or thought. To go through the drop process you can drop it, freeze it, burn it or whatever feels great and works for you. You then need to roll it into a positive emotion as quickly as possible and get into that habit so that after a while it occurs naturally.

So progressing with the negative feeling of being fat and/or unattractive, the emotion can be changed into "I'm a beautiful person with many wonderful qualities." Recognising that there are many aspects to beauty and a single factor in all those aspects does not nullify all the positive factors and your wonderful qualities.

Kinesthetic types often do move, talk and act more slowly, as they have to get a feeling for what they are doing and saying. This needs to be kept in mind when dealing with kinesthetic people. They need a bit more time to process the information and will probably not make up their minds as fast when faced with a decision or a situation especially in business.

Examples of NITs Being Changed

A common problem people have is how to change the pattern of negative thoughts. They struggle with finding the positive counterpart when their conscious mind automatically flicks to the negative thoughts repeatedly, and that is the "reality" for them. In the seminars that we have run, the same patterns emerge. However the great news is that the patterns can be changed effectively and surprisingly fast. It is also the case that you may have to fake it until you make it to change the entrenched negative thought patterns and create positive automatic thoughts in the future.

There is an old saying, "In every catastrophe, there is opportunity" – but it's up to you to find it. Therefore when things do seem bad, you need to focus on finding the positive outcome and not dwell on the negative aspects of the disaster. Take the global financial crisis, when doom and gloom swept the world. Stock markets fell dramatically and company share prices fell way below their valuations. This presented the braver investors with amazing opportunities to purchase shares below their true values, with dramatic rises in the years to follow.

John: Another example of finding opportunity in a catastrophe was when, as a young doctor, I had just bought into a practice as a partner with the requisite commercial loans and financial commitment.

How Do You Treat Your Own Negative Impulsive Thoughts?

Within six months, one of the two other partners left and then the last partner decided to leave to work for the Royal Flying Doctor Service. Unfortunately, he then demanded that I purchase the building from him at about 50% above market value with no option of negotiation, valuation or any flexibility. It seemed like a no-win situation, because if I bought the old building so far above market price, I was going to lose, and if I left the building, I would lose the patient base.

During this difficult time, I kept saying to myself, over and over, that "in every situation, there is opportunity – you just need to find it." Shortly after this crisis, another doctor across town became aware of my situation and raised the possibility of going with her to build a nice, new and purpose-built surgery in a new area of high growth. After some discussions, we agreed to join forces and built an eight-room surgery over the next few years. Remember there were only the two of us, and this seemed very ambitious. But we both had the view that we needed to get other doctors in to spread the workload and cover for holidays. This surgery was built and included all the features that we needed to run a professional practice. Amazingly over the next few years, we filled every room and the value of the property has sky-rocketed over the decades! If I hadn't been faced with the difficult decision of the practice break-up, I would never have ventured into the larger property construction and the subsequent financial and practice benefits that came with a large group practice.

Another example is when there is a power failure in the home and there is the nuisance value of not having lights, TV or computer access. The NIT-slingers will be grumpy and unhappy, while the NIT-busters will delight in lighting candles, pouring a glass of red wine and having a lovely time for communication with the whole family or a romantic meal with your loved one.

Mastering Negative Impulsive Thoughts (NITs)

Here are some NITs that we would like you to try and change into positive comments. Some options for positive alternatives include:

Table 2.   Changing NITs into PATS

NITs	PATs
I can't do it	Says who? Of course I can do it. I'll keep practising until I get it right.
That's impossible	Of course it can be done. Other people have done greater things, so I just need to work out the solution and harness my own imagination.
I am stupid	Everyone makes mistakes, and each time I attempt it, I get better and better.
He is better than I am	He is really good at that skill so I should learn from him to improve my skills in that area. We all have different areas of expertise.
Nobody likes me	Of course they like me, and with my wonderful positive thinking I will be a joy to be around.
I can't lose weight	My attempts to lose weight have not worked yet, but I just need to get the right information, put in the effort and I will succeed.
Nothing ever works out for me	This has not worked this time. What can I learn from it to have a better chance of success next time? I will get better with every attempt.

How Do You Treat Your Own Negative Impulsive Thoughts?

I always have bad luck	I make my own luck, and with a positive attitude, I will attract luck as positive thoughts attract positive outcomes.
Everyone is talking about me	I need to keep remembering that people usually act like this out of jealousy. What people want to talk about is up to them, but at least I know that I am doing the right thing, can hold my head up high. Their rumours/criticisms/comments will be shown for what they are at some time.
It's raining again so we can't go to the beach	We will still go to the beach and enjoy the rain on our face and wind in our hair.
It's so busy, I haven't had time for a lunch break	Isn't it great that it is so busy that I haven't had time for a lunch break! The business is doing really well and my job will be secure.
Seems to me I'm always waiting for him	While I know he will come home as soon as he can, I will use this time well and for my own benefit by reading a book, meditating or spending time with my friends.

It is really important for everyone to recognise and take 100% responsibility for their NITs, as these thoughts can change into words, words change into actions, actions change into habits and habits become your character. If you do not catch them early as thoughts, you pass them to others and they multiply and spread as an epidemic.

Mastering Negative Impulsive Thoughts (NITs)

Ask the questions to expose the NIT for what it is

NITs that arise in your mind often float freely through your thoughts and possibly into words without any form of filter or censor. Rather than just accepting your thoughts as acceptable because they are your own, it is a good idea to start filtering them. This will ensure the quality of your thoughts remain positive and you refuse to allow the NITs any space or power in your mind. Let's look at a few classics.

"At this rate, I'll never get to go on my holiday!" – This thought needs to challenged, and the question to neutralize this NIT would be "Really, you think you will NEVER go on holiday? Of course that is incorrect; there are just several jobs that need to be completed so I just need to get my head down and get them done!"

"Nobody likes me!" – "What, nobody in the whole world? Or is it just nobody in the whole office? The important people in my life like me, and that is much more important than these people." Or perhaps it is that nobody likes what you are doing because you are making them accountable and they don't want to be pulled into line!

"What's the point? I always fail!" – Your NITs filter needs to be picking up the pessimistic attitude and the response could be, "Do I always fail? No, of course not, so that is not correct. I have not always failed – there are many wonderful successes that I have had in the past that prove I can be successful. These recent struggles just mean that the success will be even sweeter. I need to keep on getting better and better with each attempt."

"Everyone agrees that this is a stupid way of working." – The response could be to question who amongst the involved people agree. Is it really everyone, or is it just one person with a big mouth that wants to say it's "everyone" to back themselves up? This is often the case.

How Do You Treat Your Own Negative Impulsive Thoughts?

There are often work circumstances where you may need to put a process into place that many people – or even the "everyone" in the situation – won't like. But if the whole success depends on you, then you are carrying that responsibility. If you decide this is the best process, then you make your judgment and hold your position as you will be proven right or wrong over time. If you agree with the "everyone" and put in place their process and it fails, the responsibility will be taken by "no-one," until there is a "someone" found to take the rap, and that "someone" will probably be you.

It is important to note that when you use the terms "always, never, everybody, nobody" in a negative context, it will be a NIT. However, these are great words to use when used in a positive context to empower and strengthen your resolve and encourage your ongoing efforts – e.g. the classic statements like "Never, never, never give up," "I'll always try to be the best I can be," "Nobody's responsible for where I am now except me" and "I hope everyone is inspired by my success."

So with NITs, these absolute catch-all phrases in a negative statement are an easy clue to the nature of the NIT, so watch out for them in your mind chatter and jump on them as soon as they emerge.

Make the statement to expose the NIT for what it is

Recognising the presence of a NIT is the single most important aspect in creating a NIT-free mind or a NIT-free work place or environment. Simply making a statement in your mind to label that thought as a NIT will immediately activate your personal process for the Stop, Drop and Roll process.

For a simple self-criticism like "I am looking so fat", this deserves an immediate response like "No that is a NIT. I am a wonderfully attractive and beautiful person taking active steps that I enjoy to get to the weight that I have chosen!" It is interesting that when you have put an active strategy like diet and exercise for weight loss into place, even before any weight loss is attained you will feel happier and content as you have a plan to get you to where you want to be and you know that success will follow.

If a thought pops into your head like "There is no way that I can do this job", your immediate response could be: "That is just a NIT – it is not the truth, as it is possible, and if I want to get this done, I can. It is my choice." An alternative with more detail would be "No that is just a NIT! What can I do or organise to help me get this job done? How can the process be made simpler or easier? Or who can I get to assist or do other jobs of mine to allow me to complete this more important task?"

If the thought is "This is a catastrophe. Everything is going wrong!" your mind shift in this kind of more serious situation is not to deny the challenges that you are facing but to look for solutions to the problem or opportunities that are not yet apparent. Your thoughts could go down the lines of "That statement is a NIT and absolutely unhelpful and unproductive. There certainly is a significant challenge that needs to be addressed here. So I need to see how it can be dealt with in the best way and try to look for the opportunities in this situation that I have not yet seen".

> Taking 100% responsibility for your future is very liberating, as it puts you back in the driver's seat. Remember that you alone are responsible for all of your thoughts, including your NITs. You are able to filter, censor and find the NITs, allowing you to treat and change them into positive affirmative thoughts. This will support your future progress towards your personal success and more importantly, happiness. It is in your control!

How Do You Treat Your Own Negative Impulsive Thoughts?

21-Day Rule

It has been our experience that when people become aware of a wonderful process or activity, they are so keen to spread the word and tell everyone else about it that they actively and enthusiastically spread the word. This is quite entertaining at times. We have seen individuals who have been recently exposed to meditation or yoga being so enthusiastic that they are telling everyone about what they know and how wonderful it is.

While these enthusiastic comments are done with the best intentions, the naivety of the person in this new philosophy means that they often give incorrect information or promote it to people inappropriately. In one situation, a person was telling Elizabeth that she should really "do" meditation and how you can slow your brain cycles and reduce stress in a few minutes. She had just had a couple of sessions and here was the now-expert telling Elizabeth what she should do. The irony was that Elizabeth had been performing and teaching meditation for over twenty years and had also taught meditation to this person's meditation teacher! Elizabeth was happy that her teachings were being passed on, so she just agreed with the person about how wonderful it was and reinforced the powerful effect that meditation can have.

This story shows how, as you gain more insight into NITs, the most common reaction is to go out and start telling everyone about the NITs that they are putting out or trying to educate them on what the other person needs to do. This will alienate you from the people around you and possibly annoy them. They may take it as a criticism, and the likely comeback will be that they may start to view you as a hypocrite if you haven't cleaned up your own back yard (mind) first.

So this is where the 21-day rule comes in. Work on your own internal NITs for a full twenty-one days before you start trying to deal with NITs from other people. It will be quite hard, because you will recognise the NITs in your friends and work colleagues and want to tell them to sort them out. Be patient here, and practise on yourself. The reason being, once you have had more practise at dealing with the NITs inside yourself, you will be much more forgiving to others as you realise how persistent the little blighters can be. You will protect yourself from the possible label of hypocrite. Plus you can help people more once you are more experienced at dealing with them yourself. You can use the saying "I know how you feel and it can be difficult, but what I found worked well was…"

So work only on your own NITs for twenty-one days, watching your thoughts, your words and your actions. All should be in sync, and you will find your actions and words are the easiest ones to assess while your thoughts take a bit more analysis and persistence. Don't let yourself get away with anything, as it is a habit that can only be broken by changing the habit. That NITs habit will start becoming a positive thought habit more automatically as you practise over time.

The other interesting thing to observe through this 21-day process is how much happier and more exciting things start to feel and become. Nothing may have changed, but instead of focusing your mind on the problems of life, you start to focus on the solutions and the amazing possibilities that exist. You start to see potential in situations that previously would have passed you by, and you would have lost that wonderful experience or benefit.

> Practise, practise and practise repeatedly the processes of your own NITs control, and only after you have successfully controlled your own NITs consider starting to deal with those of other people.

Summary

The Three Magic Questions will confirm the presence of NITs, and the three-step process of Stop, Drop and Roll will eliminate them. Use whatever methods work best to go through this process, whether it is visual, auditory or kinesthetic, and stop that NIT in its tracks, dropping or destroying it in some way and rolling it over into the opposite of the NIT: a PAT or Positive Affirmative Thought.

Stay alert. Always watch for NITs arising in your mind, and never let a NIT through your NIT filter! Always take 100% responsibility for where you are and where you are going. Create positive feelings when you are doing positive actions, and choose better reactions to situations that caused problems for you in the past. Yes, you can control your own thoughts!

Be patient and use the 21-day rule to practice with your own NITs before you even start to consider dealing with NITs in other people.

Let the NITs eradication begin!

6

How Do You Treat Third-Party Negative Impulsive Thoughts?

> "Without feelings of respect, what is there to distinguish men from beasts?"
> **Confucius**

Over the twenty-one day period that you have been observing your own Negative Impulsive Thoughts, we are confident that you will have started to get better at controlling them. You may have even found that they are more persistent than you thought they would be and some just keep coming back. Rest assured that practise and repetition ultimately gets them under control. We encourage you to just keep going and you will definitely get better and better at controlling all your NITs.

Isn't it amazing how common NITs are in everyday life? As you become more aware of your own NITs, you start to become aware of other people's NITs. It is incredible that so much of what you hear and see is based on NITs. In previous chapters we have talked about the abundance of NITs in the media – bad news sells newspapers and magazines. NITs are everywhere – home, workplaces, schools, social situations, religious leaders and basically life in general.

Have you had any NITs that were aimed at you personally or professionally? The initial steps for treating third-party NITs are the same as for personal ones: first you need to observe and be able to recognise them. The next step is to make sure that you protect yourself from the NITs so they don't affect you negatively – so complete the Stop, Drop and Roll treatment

Mastering Negative Impulsive Thoughts (NITs)

in your own head. Given that these NITs are already out in the community as words or actions from these other people, you do need to make sure that you don't allow yourself to continue spreading them.

Unfortunately, as the NITs are coming from other people, you have much less control over what others say and do, so unlike your own NITs, you can't necessarily step in and annihilate them immediately as this is not always socially acceptable! Give it a go if you are prepared to face World War Three, but there are easier and more successful techniques!

Don't React. Respond

It is important not to get emotionally involved when faced with third party NITs. We realise that this will take practice on your part. Reactions arise from an emotional base and in the past you would probably have instantly reacted when you were on the receiving end of a third party NITs attack. This type of emotional reaction usually results in an avalanche of escalating drama. As a result, the real issue is forgotten and quality standards that you were trying to uphold are lost. However responding comes from a values base so remember - don't react, respond.

> Therefore it is important to separate yourself from the negative emotion of the NIT **immediately** and avoid emotions of anger, frustration, disbelief, hurt or disappointment when dealing with the problem. A useful tool to create this separation is to create an imaginary glass bubble around you, and use this as a filter to choose what you allow in and what you keep out.

Another tool is the "box technique" where you see yourself taking those comments or feelings of hurt and upset, and imagine putting them in a box, wrapping it up and sealing it with rope, tape or ribbon. These NITs don't serve you in any way. All dealings with the situation need to be without an emotional overlay that will impair your judgment.

A second strategy when faced with an emotionally charged third-party NIT that will help to avoid knee-jerk reactions is to count to ten before responding. This will allow you to think through what has just been said or done. It also allows you to consider the outcomes of what you are about to do. It is better to walk away if the situation is excessively emotionally charged and this will give you more time to process your thoughts and allow you to choose an appropriate line of approach. Statements made in anger or with the knee-jerk reaction are mostly going to be counterproductive and personal in nature and very difficult to rectify later.

Interestingly when someone is being derogatory or aggressively attacking any of us, we seem to feel compelled to react immediately because we want our side of the story to be heard. The outcome of this typical reaction is a shouting match or a direct conflict where both sides are pitted directly against each other and neither is listening to each other. As tempers rise, the attacks and criticisms become personal and the original problem is forgotten. This mud-slinging match produces more and more NITs and both sides get hurt and angry and the underlying problem is still not resolved.

On the flip side, it is very liberating to realise that there are no rules requiring you to react immediately. Counting to ten or walking away gives you time to control your emotions and decide on the best response. Even if you need to physically bite your tongue while counting to ten, do it to prevent the emotional and disruptive reaction while you let the emotional intensity fade. This is of course where the expression "bite your tongue" came from. When the emotion has dissipated, you can then consider the actual problem, look for solutions and come back to the person when you are calm. In this way, you maintain your integrity, your class-act status is preserved, and you have avoided a conflict that would have escalated the problem.

John: *A great example of this was a situation where I was dealing with a patient's complaint about a doctor in the practice. As the principal of the practice, I was responsible for sorting it out. The patient complained that the doctor had treated him badly and not dealt with the medical issues that he had presented with. When I talked to the doctor in private, his immediate reaction was to become agitated, angry, tense and aggressive. Interestingly, he became aggressive and derogatory towards me, even though I was just the messenger. He was verbally abusing me and suggested that the patient should "deal directly with him if they had a problem" and how dare they doubt his decision about treatment processes?*

In reality, it was clear that this doctor's poor communication had been the problem and this aggressive reaction was a self-defence mechanism. The common reaction in that situation would be to argue the point directly with him at the time, and to defend my own integrity in the process. Potentially this would only have escalated the anger and put the two of us at loggerheads. Instead, I chose to defuse the anger and focus on the problem and totally ignore the personal remarks about me by using the **box technique**. *Having removed any personal emotional or hurtful feelings, I then had to reduce the anger and aggression coming from the doctor. Putting up both my hands, I said "Please don't shout. I am listening, so just tell me what happened so we can work out what the problem is and sort it out." I let him speak without interruption, and when he had finished, I added "Is there anything else about this that you want to add?"*

After a short reiteration of his issues, he stopped talking. I then paraphrased what he had said and asked him "Is that correct and does that cover all the issues?" This process of paraphrasing is really useful, as it lets the person know that you have heard what they have said, and also lets you know that you have understood correctly what their issues are. Many arguments arise over misunderstandings or misinterpretations of situations. Now that his issues had been stated,

How Do You Treat Third-Party Negative Impulsive Thoughts?

he was a lot more settled and less emotional, which allowed me to start addressing the original problem. "I understand how frustrating it is for you when you provide good medical services. But the patient complained about the service because of their lack of understanding of why that treatment was performed. The real problem that we need to solve here is the patient's perception of the service. Getting them the information to allow them to understand why the things were done as they were, it will then be clear for them and hopefully they will be satisfied. So what I suggest to solve the problem is to…"

It's important to reiterate the need to avoid personal emotional involvement – note that at no time did I ever go back to the NITs about myself. I just ignored them as being totally irrelevant. The next point is that you always need to "walk in the other person's shoes" and understand that their reactions are a result of how they are feeling about the situation. The doctor was feeling personally attacked at a professional level when his actions were medically fine. However it was his communication skills in explaining what was being done that had not been adequate. The patient had felt that the treatment was substandard because he didn't understand why things had been done the way they were. Walk in the other person's shoes and feel how they would feel, and many situations will be much clearer.

In this situation, I kept my integrity, kept calm, spoke even softer and slower than usual to make him have to listen to hear me and maintained my "class act". If I hadn't, potentially a major conflict could have broken out and our relationship would probably have been irrevocably damaged.

> The important strategies are to wait for the person to finish what they are saying without interruption, ask them three times if there was "anything else", paraphrase and then start addressing the issues. This gives the angry person the clear message that their issues are important to you and that you are taking them seriously, not just trying to crush them.

The technique of paraphrasing is really useful, as it has a number of benefits:

- It confirms to the other person that you were listening to them.
- It shows that you value what they were saying.
- It also allows you to summarise what you understand them to have said.
- It enables you to double-check that you have understood correctly.

Also in this situation it is critical that even if you don't believe in the other person's point of view, you need to always acknowledge that what people say is the truth for that person at that time. The perception of the doctor that he was being professionally criticised and the patient's perception that he was treated poorly were both the truth for each of those people. Trying to argue that fact in the heat of the argument with either of them is unlikely to succeed. On the other hand, finding the reason the problem has arisen will often sort it out and allow any party at fault to learn from the mistake. Failing to learn from mistakes is a much bigger fault than making the mistake in the first place, as this is one of life's fundamental personal growth processes.

In all situations where you are dealing with NITs from other people, you do need to remember that the source of all NITs is fear: fear of failure, fear of loss of reputation and (in the medical situation) fear of illness. Once you realise this fact and start to look for the underlying fear that is causing the reaction with NITs, it makes it much easier to treat the person with empathy. Plus help them to solve the problem rather than the usual reaction of ripping the person apart.

Remaining empathetic and avoiding judgmental approaches also keeps the doors open for more effective communication and problem solving. Although sometimes you will not know what the underlying fear is, you still need to manage the situation as if there is one and that person needs your help. This changes your approach from an antagonistic to a cooperative process so you get both sides working together to solve the problem.

So if you are faced with your partner saying "You're always on that computer. You think more of work than you do of me", rather than reacting emotionally with a personal attack about the cost of running the house and the stress of keeping ahead of the bills. Try saying "So what you are feeling is that I spend too much time on the computer and this makes you feel neglected. If this is correct, we need to discuss how we can get everything done that needs to be done and organise to have enough time for ourselves too!" This acknowledges the person's underlying feeling of being neglected. Plus you can start to discuss how together the two of you can organise the amount of time spent doing things together as well as work on other things apart so both parties are happy. You can even discuss how much time is necessary to get the required jobs done or options to delegate some work to other people.

The next principle is important for the more sensitive amongst us, and is about making sure that you deal with NITs that get through our defences.

Ignoring a NIT from someone else takes considerable self-confidence and a well-protected heart. For those of us who are more sensitive or vulnerable, and unable to just dismiss the NIT as rubbish and throw it away, it becomes necessary to acknowledge:

- That it is out there.
- That this is the view of that person (or that they are trying to undermine you).
- You will need to deal with it in the same way as your personal NITs: Stop, Drop and Roll.

Mastering Negative Impulsive Thoughts (NITs)

This is important to mention, as emotions that have got through your defences do need to be controlled. Just ignoring them tends to allow them to ferment, stew and gain strength. So the key to recognising that some issues or NITs are present in your mind is that it will keep popping up in your brain and repeatedly come to your attention. If this is occurring, take notice of it and deal with it properly to control and destroy it.

So in summary, the keys to dealing personally with third-party NITs are:

- Avoid emotional involvement.
- Count to 10 and bite your tongue.
- Remember what people say is the truth for them at the time.
- Keep integrity, keep calm, and maintain a class act.
- Wait for them to finish speaking, and ask if there is anything that they have missed.
- Walk in the other person's shoes to ascertain where the person is coming from.
- Remain empathetic and avoid judgment.

Managing the other people producing third-party NITs

When you are in a situation where NITs are flying around, it is important to try and negate them as soon as possible to prevent them from multiplying and gaining power. However, dealing with third-party NITs is a lot more challenging, as you do not have any direct control over the people and you can't necessarily change their behaviour. You will need to remember that although you may have influence over people in your inner circle, as the people get further and further away from you, your influence declines. With the people who are outside your influence, your strategy will be to negate the NITs that they are generating rather than trying to affect their

How Do You Treat Third-Party Negative Impulsive Thoughts?

behaviour. There may also be times that you have to choose to let their NITs go past and not do anything, as your attention to them can give them more strength.

An example of this is where a newspaper reports a story in the back pages, and when the victim of the story challenges the facts and tries to sue the paper, the ensuing newspaper coverage magnifies the effect tenfold. Unfortunately in many cases no-one ever sees the final court outcome where the victim wins. In this way everyone is left with the "knowledge" of the negative report without the knowledge of the outcome. "Throw enough mud and eventually some will stick" is the old political adage used repeatedly to undermine political opponents.

Let's discuss the processes to use when you have decided that the person generating the NITs needs to be addressed directly. All of the above information needs to be in place so you are personally protected from the NITs and are not emotionally uptight. If you are, just remove yourself or delay your response until you have had the time to decide how you want to respond. One effective technique for reducing the emotional involvement and looking at the situation differently is to say to yourself "Isn't it interesting that I find myself in this situation – what now do I need to say or do to resolve it?"

Define the problem

> Focus on working out what the problem actually is. Then make sure that it is clearly stated so everyone can focus on the actual problem and not on the personal issues that are often thrown into the verbal attack.

Anyone making personally denigrating comments should be pulled into line and advised that you are not going to deal with personal issues. For example, "I will ignore that personal attack as it doesn't help us deal with the problem that needs to be solved. The problem is…" Another option is "Let's not get into a personal mud-slinging match, as it won't help anyone. What we really need to focus on here is how to solve the problem, which is…"

Stay calm and maintain the class act, and if things get more heated, slow down even more. Speaking more softly and calmly should influence the process positively. If communication fails, then take time out and agree to discuss it later when emotions have settled. Be mindful that there are times when people are so worked up that they are unreceptive to reasonable discussion.

Communication techniques

Effective communication means that two-way communication occurs. So listening is just as important as effective speaking. The other person needs to understand what you are saying and you need to understand the other person's position. As the old saying goes, "You have two ears and one mouth, so listen twice as much as you speak." Success in life, personal contentment and effective managerial skills all require the ability to listen effectively to establish what the other person's point of view is. Then situations can be resolved to everyone's satisfaction and enable you to move to win–win outcomes.

Elizabeth: *We had a great experience of communication problems when sailing to the tropical island of Gili Trawangan in the Bali Strait between Lombok and Bali.*

There was poor anchoring and to avoid damaging the pristine reef in the crystal clear waters, we wanted to pick up a mooring. We contacted one of the local resorts, The Beach House, as they had moorings laid just off their beach. Over the VHF we got instructions and picked up the mooring after some difficulty locating it as the strong current was dragging it under the water so it could not be seen. Finally we found it, tied up the boat and in a gesture of goodwill attached one or our own floats to the buoy to give it more buoyancy and keep it on the surface. Job done, we went ashore for a meal and to see the island

How Do You Treat Third-Party Negative Impulsive Thoughts?

that absolutely lived up to its reputation as an idyllic place with no motorized vehicles and only horse drawn carts and bicycles.

At the Beach House, it took some effort to find the manager who let us use the mooring as we wanted to tell him what we had done with the extra buoy to keep it afloat. His English was good and the communication seemed to flow well. We explained about "the buoy being dragged under the water with the strong current and that to make it easier to find later, we tied on some extra rope and a second large white float to the buoy." The manager was nodding and agreeing with everything we were saying and we felt that our message was being completely understood and everything was fine: It was only right at the end of our conversation that we realised there was a serious misunderstanding. The complete lack of understanding was shown when the manager with a slight frown asked, "You know name of boy?"

Of course the keys to good communication are:

- Keep it simple and avoid double meanings, double negatives, and innuendo.

- Focus on the issue at hand and not any personal attitudes about the issue.

- Make your view on the issue clear, and if there is something that you want or you want things to be done in a certain way, be clear so that the person knows exactly what you are talking about.

- You may want to explain why things need to be done that way depending on the relationship with that person (partner, child, boss, junior), but the key is to be specific with instructions. For example, "Please make sure that the phones are answered in three rings" rather than "Please answer the phones quickly."

○ Focus on the positives in the situation. If a single problem has arisen in a process, don't focus only on the single problem but remind everyone how he or she is doing so well with all the other processes. Build them up emotionally before discussing the "area where some improvement could be seen" or the area "where things aren't going as smoothly as we would like."

○ After discussing the problem, restate how well the other areas are running so the focus of the problem is balanced or sandwiched with positives on both sides. The natural tendency to only focus on the problem gives everyone the idea that "everything is a catastrophe" or that "we are all doing such a terrible job". It is more often the case that the correction is a very small part of the whole system that overall is going very well, so make sure that this emphasis is conveyed in your discussions.

It has been stated to us many times by friends or patients that they don't know how doctors deal with the terrible things that happen to patients sometimes, despite their best efforts. This is a NIT, because while doctors are trained to heal people and help them live, doctors also need to ensure that as people die, they are at peace, maintain dignity and avoid suffering.

Elizabeth: *A dramatic example of this was when John, our two sons and I were doing aid work in the remote islands of Vanuatu in the South Pacific with Project MARC (Medical Assistance to Remote Communities). John was the lead doctor of a team of younger doctors and aid workers and we were travelling by boat to the isolated islands providing medical services to the villages where no facilities existed. In one of the most northern groups of Vanuatu, there is a gorgeous island called Hui, where the local tribes had seen white people occasionally but they had never seen white children at all. Our kids were treated like royalty and encouraged to join in at school, where they learned how to make bows and arrows, chop down coconuts and open them with machetes.*

How Do You Treat Third-Party Negative Impulsive Thoughts?

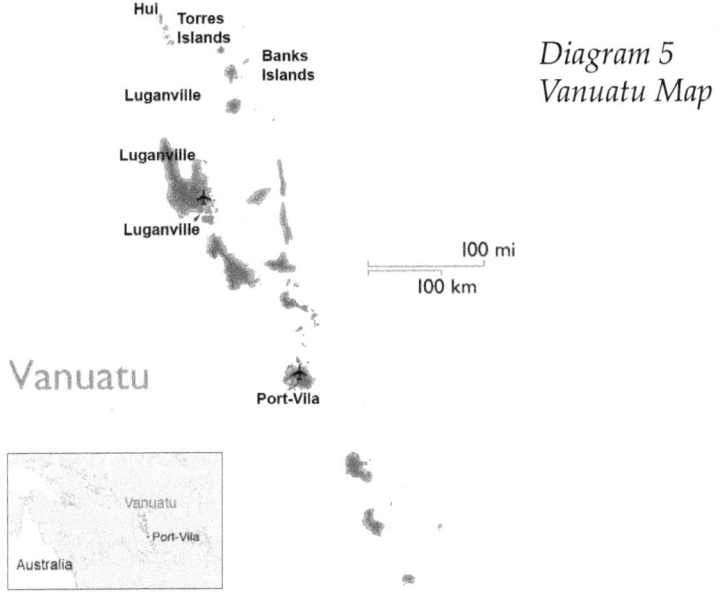

Diagram 5
Vanuatu Map

In this tropical paradise, John was asked to go and see an old man called Jonas who was bed-bound, dying and in severe pain. After getting the story in the local pigeon English language and examining him, it was clear that he had a completely obstructed bladder so was unable to pass any urine. He had been in this condition for some time, and as a result his lower abdomen was swollen like a watermelon and, of course, he was in severe pain. His family didn't know the extent of his illness or what was wrong with him, and this once-strong tribal elder was a wasted skeleton of a man.

The whites of his eyes were a dull yellow from the illness and you could see the fear and distress in his eyes from the unrelenting pressure in his abdomen, the fine tremor in his hands and beads of sweat trickling down his body. The underlying problem was almost certainly cancer of the prostate or bladder, with infection and complete obstruction to the bladder. In developed countries, as an acute emergency this would be rapidly treated with catheterisation, but all we had with us were medications as surgical-type intervention was not expected on this trip.

Mastering Negative Impulsive Thoughts (NITs)

It was obvious to John what Jonas's fate was, and that his role was now purely palliative. It was clear, however, that some of the junior doctors had trouble coping with the prospect of not being able to save his life. They were suggesting urgent airlift to the nearest hospital for more active and aggressive treatment, but clearly this view came from the limited experience of these younger doctors who had not been faced with the need to accept that their skill is sometimes to help the patient to die – preferably pain-free and with dignity. It would certainly not be the patient's desire to be separated from his family, his home and his support with only a short time to live. Later that evening, John used this real-life situation to expand the junior doctors' minds and to help them understand that their role includes helping terminally ill people die in the environment of their choice, in peace and with dignity.

So what to do with Jonas? He was started on antibiotics and painkillers, but the only way to alleviate his pain was by draining his bladder. There was no room for NITs to pop in, like "We have no equipment," "There is nothing we can do" or "It is beyond our ability." This gent needed urgent decompression of the bladder to get some relief, so John went back to the yacht and looked around for something that could be made into a catheter. We needed flexible rubber tubing about the diameter of a pencil. However, there was nothing on board in the medical supplies, kitchen, chart table or spare parts. So after searching in the engine compartment, he found a fuel pipe about the right thickness, cut a section off and reconnected the remainder so the engines still worked. John then fashioned the end to suit the purpose, cleaned and sterilised it, and made his way back to Jonas; hoping that he would be able to get the tube past whatever was blocking the bladder outlet. John explained what he needed to do and Jonas agreed without hesitation. I crossed my fingers as John asked for some divine assistance and started.

So there we were in a straw hut, with a man on a leaf mat on the dirt floor in the semi-dark, using a fuel pipe in extremely unsterile conditions trying to force through a very resistant obstruction. Jonas' eyes grew wide due to the increased pain, but he never let out a whimper as John forced the tube further inwards. All of sudden the tube passed the blockage and thick green pus gushed from the tube into the bowl that I was holding. The stench was overwhelming and I involuntarily lurched backwards.

John took the bowl from me as I stepped back with all the others away from the smell, leaving John alone with his head close over the bowl of pus. This meant that he was now operating single-handedly, holding the bowl and the catheter tube and trying to massage the abdomen all at the same time. Clearly John was struggling to suppress his own violent urge to vomit as well, and he had to crouch on his haunches for a long time, head low over the abdomen. Staying in this awkward position meant that John's legs were becoming painful and going numb, and I could see that John had to put all of his own discomfort aside and keep his focus on Jonas' needs. The green liquid just kept on oozing out, and the old man's face softened as his bladder size reduced. John had to continue massaging the bladder for some time to try and get as much out as possible before removing the tube.

John had to return every day to repeat the procedure, as the bladder would not drain by itself and the pus in the bladder was continuing to build up each day, despite the antibiotics. Each day, I witnessed an incredible display of humility and humanity as I saw Jonas looking up with gratitude to John as he performed the procedure... Once in a lifetime, you witness something that has a major effect on your emotions, and that scene of Jonas and John exchanging glances of gratitude and understanding, without any words being spoken, will stay with me as the most incredible and selfless gift that one person can give to another. It was inspiring!

Consider Visual, Auditory and Kinesthetic

When you have to discuss more complicated problems or issues relating to NITs from third parties, use the communication form that suits each of their personalities. You may like to refer to chapter 5 and the descriptions of visual, auditory or kinesthetic. Obviously you need to pay attention to how the other person operates to work out their communication type.

Only then can you use the terms and phrases that they will respond to and understand best. So in discussions use terms like "I see your problem", "I hear what you are saying" or "I understand how you must feel." These are useful for the visual, auditory and kinesthetic people respectively, and they will understand much better if you keep the analogies along these lines.

Another communication strategy to help deal with NITs is to ask questions. If you are trying to negate NITs, useful questions include:

- "Why do you feel/think that?"
- "What makes you believe that?"
- "Where did you get that information?"
- "Is that information confirmed to be the truth?"

Keep asking and go deeper and deeper into the source of the comment. That will often get to the underlying problem that shows the lack of truth or exposes the true emotion behind the statements. The person asking the question has to remain uninvolved emotionally and not get drawn in to an argument about the truth or otherwise of each piece of information. This process is very useful as it does allow you to remain non-judgmental. After all, you are only asking questions to obtain more detail and you have provided no input into the subject at all. This way no-one can accuse you of taking sides, passing judgment or agreeing with the NITs. It also allows the person who is giving out the information to be heard. Plus you are supporting them by asking for more details to try and find out all the exact details of the information, which in turn allows you to find out the degree of truth and the sources involved.

If the problem has been defined and it remains unclear to you what the person is trying to achieve in the situation, you would need to ask some key phrases such as:

How Do You Treat Third-Party Negative Impulsive Thoughts?

- "How do you believe I can help you?"
- "Do you think there is anything I can do to help solve this for you?"
- "I am certainly open to trying to find a solution to this with you."

These statements are open and neutral statements without being judgmental in a negative or positive way, but will allow you to see what the person wants to achieve in the situation.

This is establishing what the person's expectations are for a solution to the situation without emotional overlay, and allows you to clearly see if they know what they want – and sometimes they won't! It also puts the focus on finding the solution rather than restating over and over what the problem is and getting more and more emotional or upset about the problem. It is also a non-confrontational way to deal with the situation, although relatively time-consuming. These skills are very useful to develop for negotiating processes as moving the other person to understanding the errors of their thought processes, while not actually challenging them, is a key technique for any first-class negotiator or sales person!

John: An interesting experience relating to the importance of listening and identifying the real problem happened when I was doing aid work in a leprosy mission in Nepal. We were treating all levels of people disabled by the disease. The more severe form, called lepromatous, causes the loss of the nose, fingers and toes and even limbs if not treated. Many of these patients were beggars and were visibly deformed. Antibiotics can now cure both forms of leprosy, but require many months of treatment.

What I struggled to understand, was why these beggars were repeatedly coming back for treatment and not just taking the tablets until they were better. This was one of my lessons in avoiding judgment – with my naïve Western standards, my logic was saying; just take the tablets until you are healed! When I started to listen and imagine what they had to deal with, it became more obvious. If they completed their treatment and were cured, they would lose their ability to beg and no-one would employ someone that had clearly been a leper. As a result, their families would starve because of the absence of social security.

The solution for them was therefore to treat their leprosy when it started to get too bad, but cease treatment before they got too healthy. Once the wider implications were seen and their position was understood, the answer was no longer quite so simple!

Lesson learned: don't judge, and be a better listener!

Direct challenge to the NITs

The process of talking someone through from their NIT-based position to a more positive attitude, without directly challenging them, is time-consuming but essential in some delicate situations. Where you do not have the time, or if the circumstances are appropriate, you can directly challenge the statement or highlight its nature as being untrue, unhelpful, negative or inappropriate. Remembering that this will result in a confrontational situation where the other person may take offence or fight back. Skill and good judgment is very strongly advised for it to be done successfully without negative outcomes.

> The blunt approach may be appropriate at times, using a statement like "I am sorry but I don't agree with that statement" and then giving the reasons. Alternatively you can:
>
> - contradict the NITs just released as being either untrue if you know that to be the case.
> - make the statement that it is unhelpful if it is in the work or group situation.
> - if people in the conversation know the NIT principle, you can just label it as a NIT.

How Do You Treat Third-Party Negative Impulsive Thoughts?

This is fast, effective and can have good results when used in the right situation, but sometimes if the person is sensitive or your senior, you may need to soften the direct challenge. The techniques to contradict a NIT in a softer and more conciliatory fashion could be to use the following:

- "Interesting that you see it that way, as I believe…"
- "Have you considered…?"
- "Are you willing to consider…?"

Clearly all these direct approaches leave the clear stated position that you hold, which puts you clearly on one side of the fence in any dispute. This is fine if you are happy to have your choice of sides being public. In some cases this may well be important and preferable (for instance if there are standards or propriety under threat), but if you are trying to move someone from their set position to your position in sales or principle discussions, then direct challenging would not be the right approach.

Let's look at some real-life examples of negating NITs from third parties. To a comment in the workplace like "This new system is useless and is not going to work and everyone agrees with me," the response could be "Really? Everyone agrees? I am sure that if I ask around, that is not the general opinion. Now let's have a closer look at why you don't think this system is going to work. This is a good system, but perhaps you don't understand all of the detail and reasons for it to be used."

To a NIT like "Jo Bloggs is just useless at doing his job and means the rest of us have to wait and he holds everything up," the response could be "Our workplace looks for all staff to support and help each other. Let's look to find out what the problem really is so that it can be solved before blaming Jo. If these things that you say are actually happening then Jo may need extra training or perhaps that job can't be done by one person alone." In fact, in this situation Jo was not being given the information in time so other people were accusing him unfairly.

Mastering Negative Impulsive Thoughts (NITs)

"This meeting will be a waste of time" is a NIT that will undermine all possibility of the meeting having good outcomes. A helpful response could be "Perhaps you could think about changing that comment into a helpful one that improves the situation, not worsens it. It is the responsibility of all of us to work out what we all need to do to get this meeting to have useful outcomes."

"These rules/protocols/requirements are ridiculous!" could be addressed with "Isn't it interesting that you should view this quality control as ridiculous when they are there to ensure things are done properly for the good of the company."

For a personal NIT of someone else in the group like "I know for a fact that those two people are having an affair within this company and it's disgusting," could be negated with "If you want to have that opinion, it is probably better to keep it to yourself no matter how much or how little truth there is in it. We don't spread gossip in this company and it's none of our business what they do outside of work. Especially if it does not affect their work performance."

For a NIT such as "Our opposition runs rings around us" could be addressed with "If you can't think of something positive or constructive to say, it would be better to say nothing! However, if there is any truth in that statement then how can we improve things, because all of us, including yourself, are responsible for improving services to be equal to or even better than the competition."

If a third-party NIT crosses your path that denigrates you with personal criticism about your looks, integrity, work ethic or other features, you may have to fall back on affirmation or thoughts of "I am a great person with wonderful qualities. What a shame that these people don't recognise those qualities and appreciate me. I will have to find a group of people to call my friends that share the same values."

How Do You Treat Third-Party Negative Impulsive Thoughts?

If you needed to deal with these comments publically, you would probably be better off giving facts and figures that show your qualities and work ethic. For example, "What a shame someone thinks so badly of me when I have been working tirelessly in the community to help the homeless/sick/children. It must be that these people spreading these malicious and inaccurate rumours have some spiteful reason to undermine my success! What a shame that they feel the need to do that, as it seems to be the tall poppy syndrome."

Of course the other alternative when dealing with malicious NITs from third parties is just to continue doing such wonderful work or achieving such success that is seen by so many people that the NIT-slingers are discredited. "The best revenge is to live well!"

Avoidance strategies

The opposite choice to dealing with the NITs directly is to completely avoid dealing with it. This option can let the NIT quietly run out of steam and just die a natural death. Or it may be coming from people or groups that are outside of your influence or your respect, so their opinions are of no consequence. If over time these NITs start to gain traction, power or influence, you may have to reverse that decision and deal with them directly.

When faced with NITs that you are choosing to ignore, immediate comments may well be along these lines:

- "Whatever thoughts they have about me are none of my business!"
- "Let's keep our opinions about each other to ourselves and deal with the problem at hand."
- "I avoid getting involved in gossip, so with all due respect, I will ignore those comments."
- "I'm sorry I can't get involved; it's against my

religion!" (In a joking manner)
- "It's really none of my business because no one knows the whole story."
- "I'm not going to play God and make a judgment on that as I'm not perfect either."
- "Perhaps we need to put ourselves in their shoes to get a full understanding of what's going on."

Surround yourself with positive people

"Surround yourself with only people who are going to lift you higher", was one of Oprah Winfrey's quotes, and is an established success principle. This strategy has the dual action of preventing you from getting dragged down and actively boosting you to higher levels of success.

It is about choosing your friends, workplace, associates and employees wisely and trying to surround yourself with optimistic people who will reinforce positivity and avoid NITs. It is much easier to maintain a positive and NIT-free environment when you have people around you who share the same outlook in life.

Alternately, you will find that some people just revel in creating drama and NITs abound in their company all the time. It is as if their life is only "good" when they have problems and drama to deal with. If their life is going smoothly and pleasantly, they create problems out of seemingly nothing or make arguments and drama out of something small and minor. We all know people like this, and you can see how these people create chaos and drama in life even though sometimes it is artificially created with exaggeration, embellishment or complete misrepresentations of the truth – in other words, lies!

If people like this form large sections of your social circles, this may be the reason why your life is full of chaos and drama. You will need to consider teaching these individuals about

How Do You Treat Third-Party Negative Impulsive Thoughts?

NITs so they can reduce their NIT production or associate with different people. Sorry, but this is a real choice, and sometimes you will find dropping some people from your life can dramatically improve the quality of your life. We have done this personally, when it has become obvious that certain people are not on the same page as us. These people were just creating unnecessary drama all the time that kept our focus away from the wonderful things in our life that we preferred to focus our attention on.

Create a NIT-free environment around you

In all your family, work and social environments, it is important to move everyone towards having a NIT-free approach to life. If you can start spreading the word, others will start multiplying the good stuff and limiting the NITs around you. Talking to your family and children about NITs, pulling them up and correcting them, will start getting them into NIT-free habits. If they start to spread the word and neutralise their own NITs, it gets easier for you.

In the workplace, having the whole group educated about NITs is helpful in making the environment NIT-free, but if that has not happened, talk to people one at a time, share this book with others, give it as present to your boss (he or she will eventually get to this line and realise where the idea came from) and consider organising NIT training for the workplace.

One serious warning that you will need to look at and consider over time, is to watch what sort of environment you have at home, especially with regards to the choice of TV programs, movies and games that you watch. If you come away from a movie or program feeling washed out, drained, uptight and anxious, then perhaps you should consider limiting how much exposure you have to these programs. There are many programs that are enlightening, empowering and of a general feel-good nature. We have stressed this in previous chapters and we are stressing it again – this is very important.

Our view is that real day-to-day life is full of enough challenges and burdens, so why expose yourself to extra unnecessary emotionally taxing negative drama?

Just be happy – you will live longer!

Summary

The key to treating third-party NITs is for you to avoid personal emotional involvement in the NIT that is being circulated; remain neutral about it and gather more information. Define early on what the actual problem is, so that everyone can focus on the problem and avoid making it a personal attack against any individual. Keep your own integrity and use communication terms that are non-judgmental.

There are two approaches to dealing with the third-party NITs: Direct contradiction or more subtly working around the issue to prove its lack of validity. The individual situation will determine which of these is most appropriate. Avoidance strategies can also be used if the NIT can be ignored and left to wither and die a natural death, making sure that they do not gain momentum over time.

Surround yourself with positive people and create a NIT-free environment in your relationships, home, workplace and wider community. Spreading the word and increasing people's awareness about NITs will make all of our lives happier and healthier!

7
How Do You Create Great Life Habits?

> "The only difference between 'Try' and 'Triumph' is a little Umph!"
> **Marvin Phillips**

When trying to change habits, the mind will naturally resist, as the established status quo is the preferred option for your subconscious. It is easier and more comfortable for the mind to accept things as they are, even if they are not necessarily the best for you. The trick with changing habits is to be clear about the habit that you need to eliminate as well as choosing an alternative habit to replace the old one. You will find that removing the old habit and leaving an empty space just doesn't work. You also need to keep persisting and reinforcing the new habit until this becomes the new status quo. It's a bit like learning to type, once you can stop thinking where the keys are, you can focus on the words and the habit just occurs automatically.

Whilst these habit-breaking processes are being used here to get you out of the NITs habit, the same processes can be used for any habit in your life. In this chapter we will be looking at breaking habits by using affirmations, laughter, mentors and anchors with visualisations so that you will have several effective NIT busting strategies.

Using affirmations to change NITs habits

Affirmations have been used for centuries for motivation and self-confidence. They are short positive phrases or sentences, which have been proven as essential for high-performance athletes, who rely on them for their success. Affirmations are used to eliminate thoughts of self-doubt and lack of confidence, which you can now recognise as NITs. The opposite of a NIT is a Positive Affirmative Thought (PAT). Because the mind controls your future success in life, it is just as important to train your mind as it would be to train your body, if you were trying to be a successful athlete.

Affirmations will work for both individuals and teams or groups. With individuals, the focus is on improving their own self belief and performance. For team or group activities, belief in the "team" and trust in each team member is critical for success and affirmations will create this unified approach.

An example of this is a football team getting psyched up for a grand final. Obviously, both teams are fit and skilled at the top level of their sport. There will usually be joint chanting or hand-gathering to represent unity and mutual support. The crowd also has a chant and team "war cry", which reinforces the team unity and belief that they will triumph. Everyone knows that the home team has an advantage, because of the NITs and self-doubt in the opposing team. However, the team that has the most self-belief and conviction will be much more likely to win.

Many high-performing teams use joint visualisations of their team performing as a smooth, efficient single unit in the build-up to competition, and combine this with affirmations of mutual self-belief and trust.

Within your personal life, affirmations are natural and occur more often than you may realise. For example, when you are going to a meeting with your boss, giving a talk in front of people or starting a new job, you will find yourself saying "I can do this; I will be fine, I am a great presenter." Or when approaching the boss for a pay rise, your thoughts may be "I do a great job, I am worthy of more money. Look at the benefits I bring to the company." All of these thoughts are affirmations that you have been thinking quite naturally. Obviously they help your emotional state at the time, but they also definitely work.

Let's look at the process of integrating affirmations into your regular lives to eliminate NITs and create a happy and healthy attitude towards life. For any person faced with daily challenges, affirmations are a great way of reprogramming their negative responses to life. Negative thinking is just a habit, and affirmations can be used to create the alternative positive habit to replace it.

> The one key that is essential to making affirmations work is that you need to link a strong emotional reaction and belief to the affirmation. In the past when people tell us that "affirmations don't work," in delving a bit deeper, we have established that the emotional connection was absent.

The emotion is the key because it's the emotion that unlocks the subconscious to allow the negative belief to be replaced with the positive one. The more emotion you can attach to the affirmation, the more powerful it will become. You can also use that strong and positive emotion to be your motivating driver on your path to your success.

It is important to think of yourself as already having achieved that success, and as that successful person, your behaviour matches that achievement and self-perpetuates. This means that even though you have not yet lost all the weight, you think, feel and act like you already have and consequently make life choices to match that achievement, like eating healthier foods and keeping physically active. If your goal is to be a successful businessperson, you would be dressing, speaking, behaving and acting like a successful businessperson even though you may still be low down on the ladder. Very interesting things will happen when everyone around you acknowledges that you are destined for higher things!

Affirmations can be used anywhere and anytime, but the best times are early in the morning when your mind is fresh and more receptive to the new concepts and as you are going off to sleep.

Affirmation exercise for positive habit changes

Stand in front of the mirror and establish which NITs are standing in the way of your personal desires or dreams. Formulate a short sentence that contains key words that conjure up strong, important feelings and outcomes for you. This is going to become your motto or affirmation. These sentences need to be stated in the present tense, as if you are already there, as these trigger your subconscious to attract those positive outcomes. If you struggle with belief in the words at the start, you have to "fake it until you make it!" Just keep repeating the statements with emotion and imagine how it would feel to already be there! Here are some examples of positive affirmative thoughts (PATS) - affirmations:

- "I open myself to all positive opportunities in my life."
- "I am a wonderful, positive person and I am open to all the great opportunities that come my way."
- "I love my world, which is surrounded by positive people and events that complete my happiness."
- "I am very positive and positive attracts positive."
- "My thoughts are positive, my actions are positive, my future is spectacular!"
- "As a fantastic positive person, I attract like-minded people and opportunities to create my ideal world."

How Do You Create Great Life Habits?

Choose a phrase that best suits you (or make a better one yourself), write it down on a piece of paper, and stick it on the mirror. Women can also write it in lipstick across the top of the mirror so that it is always in front of you when you get up. Repeat the phrase slowly to yourself and turn the words over in your mind, slowly enough so that you can feel each word. Repeat it several times slowly in your mind, gradually generating stronger feelings towards the affirmation. Just imagine what it would be like if it was true, and how that would feel, and then build on that feeling. There only needs to be a small spark of excitement at the start, and you can gradually magnify the feeling.

When you start to get a feeling of excitement in your stomach, start speaking the words out aloud. Start softly at first and then increase the volume to magnify the feeling more and more. Repeat this several times until you are buzzing with conviction and excitement and have the feeling magnified to a strong level. At first you may only get the feeling up to a 4 or 5/10, but as you practise and improve, you will be able to get up to a 10/10 even if that means that you have to act it up. Throw your arms in the air and declare with such determination that even the dog is convinced! You can use this process at any time to pick yourself up and to get you back to this point before major events like presentations, performances or even going to sign up to the gym for the first time.

Repeat this every morning, as it will reinforce to your subconscious and conscious mind the underlying beliefs and desires. This gives you a great kick-start to the day, making you feel empowered and energised. The doctor's affirmation prescription is therefore:

"Affirmation – repeat 20 times loudly and slowly with strong emotion. Use every morning and at other times if required.

Warning: unbelievable success and life benefits will occur. If pain persists, increase the dose!"

Laughter is the best medicine

Many studies have been carried out over the years that prove the beneficial effects and the power of laughter and how it affects the human body and mind. William Fry, Professor at Stanford University, proved that it has many benefits including:

- Inducing a feeling of well-being and euphoria.
- The release of the feel-good hormones of encephalins and endorphins which also act as natural pain killers.
- Improved immunity with increased activity of the T cells that are our infection scavengers.
- Lowering of levels of the stress hormone cortisol; which makes you gain weight and thins your bones.

Separate research has found that laughter also improves sugar control in diabetics, and the list of benefits continues to grow as more and more research is done into the subject.

Elizabeth: I was brought up in a family where humour was second nature, with laughing the most common sound echoing through our big house. When a bad situation arose and the mood turned melancholy, someone within the family would do their best to lighten the mood and cheer the others up by pointing out the funny side of the situation. This would usually start with my father and progress to all participating in the comedy, each person adding to the topic and one joke being outdone by the next. So I for one, have always believed in the power of laughter, as I saw how beautifully it worked.

In my quest to explore natural modalities and add more power to the skills I was already using, I jumped at the opportunity to learn the new phenomena that was sweeping the planet called Laughing Yoga. I looked into the theory and the science behind the process, and found that Laughing Yoga was the brainchild of Dr Madan Kataria, who himself was a physician researching the effects of laughing for the betterment of his own patients. He designed and compiled a course where the participants spent the best part of an hour laughing at nothing at all. As part of the course, we learned how little we laugh in life, how conditioned we had become to suppress most of our emotions – both happy and sad ones – and became aware of the need to let emotions out in a positive way.

I was fine with the theory part of the course, but when the time came to put all those laughing techniques into practice, I realised that even though I thought of myself as being quite humorous and quite open, I started to struggle doing the warm-up exercises. These consisted of saying "Hahaha, hohoho, very good! Very good! Yeah!" along with clapping out the rhythm and giving the thumbs-up sign with the "Yeah!" There I was, a trained professional, feeling as though I was in the middle of a kindergarten class. I could feel my face becoming red with embarrassment and my stomach getting tighter. The more the teacher was being animated and trying to get the group to participate, the more ridiculous it seemed and the less involved I felt.

I was surrounded by seemingly enthusiastic participants, who only made me feel even more like a fish out of water, but it only got worse. We then had to start faking laughter, acting out strange things like hiding behind our hands and saying "Peek-a-boo," then throwing our heads back and forcing out a laugh. After that, we had to stand around in a circle with everyone pretending to laugh really hard, but there was a catch: You had to do it silently! Can you imagine this was just the warm-up?

So as you would expect, the NITs in my head were coming in thick and fast: "Oh my God, what have I got myself into? This has to be the worst decision. I have spent hundreds of dollars for this course, flights, accommodation, lost income from my normal job, and to top it all off I am spending the best part of a week with these weirdos."

At this point, I realised that I had to make a conscious choice of either running for it at the next tea break, or just sticking it out to see if I could take something positive from the experience! I was way out of my comfort zone, and the natural response options to that is fight or flight. Could I escape at the next break? Would anyone notice?

Mastering Negative Impulsive Thoughts (NITs)

I looked to the right of me and really started to pay attention to the rest of the group. Locking eyes briefly with several of them and observing their body language, I realised they were feeling exactly the same as I was: Their eyes were wide with expressions of "Oh my God, have I really paid to do this? This is absurd! Let the earth swallow me up!" They were feeling the absurdity and awkwardness of the situation too, and at this stage NITs were rampant and everyone was struggling with their internal battles.

Glancing to my left, I spotted Steve, the conservative lawyer. His doctor had advised him to take up a new hobby to relieve his stress levels, so here he was trying to relieve stress, but this really was not helping! His eyes were as wide as saucers, like a deer caught in headlights and he was avoiding eye contact from embarrassment and obviously thinking "I can't believe I'm doing this! Ridiculous, what a waste! I hope no-one finds out, my reputation will be ruined!"

He was externally trying to be OK with these warm-up movements and the get-ready-to-laugh exercises, but I could sense the turmoil he was feeling inside. He suddenly realised that I was looking at him, and our eyes met and silently we both rolled our eyes with the realisation that we all felt the same way. At this point I could not contain my sense of humour any longer, and with a convulsive blurt, I let out hysterical laughing from somewhere deep in my belly.

It wasn't until then that I experienced how powerful laughter really is, with its ability to relieve stress and negativity, give self-confidence and prevent us from taking ourselves too seriously. The laughter flushed away the stressful feelings in exactly the same way that exercise does, which works in a similar way - releasing the feel-good hormones and burning off the adrenaline and cortisol. The waves of laughter were associated with waves of euphoria washing over me, even though it was artificially stimulated and there was not really anything funny happening.

I spent the next few days laughing harder than I can remember in my adult life and learnt a great deal about myself and others that week. It reminded me of how I was as a child, and that I would just laugh

How Do You Create Great Life Habits?

a lot, not because something was particular funny, but because I was happy.

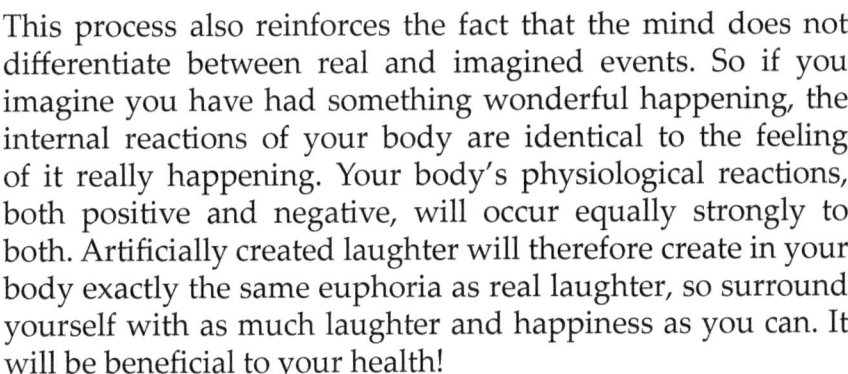

This process also reinforces the fact that the mind does not differentiate between real and imagined events. So if you imagine you have had something wonderful happening, the internal reactions of your body are identical to the feeling of it really happening. Your body's physiological reactions, both positive and negative, will occur equally strongly to both. Artificially created laughter will therefore create in your body exactly the same euphoria as real laughter, so surround yourself with as much laughter and happiness as you can. It will be beneficial to your health!

The opposite is also unfortunately true. Major stress events having been shown to lead to serious illnesses. In clinical practice, it has been repeatedly noted that after major emotional traumas, serious illnesses often occur like breast cancer, bowel cancer, heart attacks and strokes. We often see previously healthy people die without any medical explanation soon after the death of their beloved spouse. This is loosely put down to dying of a "broken heart", but is medically unexplained.

Remember that watching terrible events on the TV, movies or news will also create negative emotion and reactions as if you are personally involved. Your body goes through all the physiological reactions to stress, with the resulting raised blood pressure, fast heart, sweating, shaking, stress, adrenaline and cortisol release – but you have been sitting still. So you have been getting all the bad effects of negativity and stress on your body without the balancing effects of exercise!

Negative inputs to your emotional state without any effective release are bad for your health and well-being. So you should be very selective as to what you are regularly exposing your mind and body to and choose your programs carefully. Laughter, love-making and exercise are wonderful releases of pent-up stress and negativity and are three important keys to releasing stress from the body.

Interesting research from 1993 by Dr Backster in the US Army, shows that negative emotions cause our DNA to change. They removed people's saliva containing skin cells and the DNA could be seen to unravel when the person experienced strong negative emotion by being shown videos. Even more surprising, was that when the DNA was moved to the next room, a building a few hundred metres (yards in the US) or several hundred miles away, the effect is the same and instantaneous. This has all been wonderfully described by Gregg Braden in The Divine Matrix, and reinforces what we see in clinical practice.

> This explains why negative emotions can lead to cancer from the DNA changes but it raises more questions about the physics and what is the connection to our DNA over long distances that have not yet been explained by anyone! Amazing stuff.

Laughter exercise

Here is an exercise that will allow you, within minutes, to change your feelings from bad or sad to feeling happy and invigorated. It shows how you can artificially change your body's responses and proves that you don't have to be a victim of feeling bad. This is one tool to have in your emotional toolbox to use anytime you need it.

Sit quietly in a comfortable position and take in some slow deep breaths for a minute or so, slowing your heart rate down. Say the word "Relax" over and over in your mind as you breathe out, allowing your eyes to close. Be aware that your body is comfortable and your breathing is slower. Use your imagination and your memory to take you back to a time or event that you remember as being exceptionally funny.

How Do You Create Great Life Habits?

Play the event over in your mind, recalling the details of the event and how hilarious it was, how it made you feel and how everyone was in stitches of laughter. Go back over the event in slow motion to get all the details of the event. Picture the colours really vividly in your mind and turn up the volume of the event so you can hear all the details and take yourself back to the time and place where it was happening. See who was there; hear what was being said, what happened and how you felt.

Remember why this was the most hilarious thing you have ever seen and how the laughter bubbled up inside of you until you had no control but to laugh out loud. See yourself laughing out loud, hear yourself laughing, and relive that moment. Go over this funny event in your mind as many times as necessary until you feel the laughter and happiness bubbling up inside of you and allow yourself to laugh out loud as the event replays in your mind.

This is a fantastic stress-relief process. It's guaranteed to help and it's free! Practise the exercise, as the more you do it, the better you become at it.

The secret weapon of the rich and famous: anchoring positive feelings

Anchoring is a process that allows you to easily reproduce the feelings of positive emotion at any time. So if you have just been practising the laughter exercise and have built yourself up to having that wonderfully happy and enthusiastic feeling, using an anchor will allow you to generate that feeling quickly and without having to go through the whole exercise again.

It can also be used to immediately return the person to a place of calmness, self-confidence, peak performance or motivation, depending on what the person requires at any point in time. This technique is used by many psychologists and NLP (Neuro-linguistic Programming) practitioners in clinical practice, and also by public speakers, elite sports people, politicians and high-profile people who have to perform under pressure and deal with situations in a positive way.

Imagine you have had a very stressful day and tonight you are to host an important event, but you are definitely not in the right frame of mind. You will have to be the life and soul of the party, entertaining the guests and showing everyone a good time. You can't cancel and you know that if you don't calm down, relax and change your mood, the outcome will definitely not be positive. This is where you can use your anchor to trigger earlier emotions of happiness and hilarity so that you can mirror that state prior to going into this event.

The process is the same: you need to get yourself into the state of overwhelming laughter and happiness, and on a scale of one to ten, you need to be off the scale – let's say aim for fifteen! For the anchor to work, you need to build and magnify the feeling so that you are almost bursting with its magnitude. You need to turn up the colour and volume of the funny situation to get the score as high as it can be. When you think you are at the top of the score, you need to double it! Keep magnifying the feeling until it is at fever pitch and you are at a peak.

Only when you are at your peak do you apply your anchor. Doing it early will make it less effective and therefore have less benefit in the future. So build up the power of the feelings over and over before applying the anchor. The anchor can be any gesture that you can perform at any time without it being too obvious, like applying pressure to your left palm with your right thumb, pulling at your ear lobe or biting down on your tongue. At the point of the emotional peak, perform the anchor for 10-15 seconds. You can repeat this exercise many times to reinforce or reactivate the anchor in the future, especially if the effect is wearing off over time. This is called "stacking" anchors, and it is just a reinforcement process.

How Do You Create Great Life Habits?

You will then associate the emotional feeling of euphoria with the physical anchor, which you should now be able to trigger by repeating the action. So if your anchor was pressing your palm, at any time you can press your palm for the 10-15 seconds and you should feel the waves of euphoria and happiness flowing over you to move you to recreate that feeling again.

If the anchor does not work, it may be that your peak of emotion was not strong enough, you activated it at the wrong time, or you didn't activate the anchor in the same manner. If it doesn't work or only works slightly, just go back and go through the exercise again to reinforce and strengthen the effect.

Elizabeth: A personal example of eliciting an anchor when I need to get back to a state of calm and focus is a time when I had just had a frightening accident in my car. The glass from the window was broken and shattered into my face, cutting me just above the eye. I was on my way to work at the surgery, as I was counseling a woman who was very upset over the breakup of her marriage, and she needed to see me regularly at this traumatic time of her separation. I drove to work feeling the warm blood running down my face, John was at the hospital so I saw another doctor in the practice who managed to extract the glass and join my skin back together.

I had around five minutes to compose myself before the consult with the woman in distress. This was the moment I had to call on my anchor – I clasped my hands together for 15 sec and waited for the waves of calm and focus to wash over me while I took long deep breaths and slowed my heart rate down. I managed to centre myself enough that after the session, the women I had been counselling said that she had really benefitted greatly from that particular session. It was only on the way out that she noticed and inquired about what had happened to my face. I remained professional and said it was just a scratch and that it looked worse than it really was, although I had been suppressing the stinging pain throughout the session. I was therefore able to do what was needed by using the anchoring techniques to both calm and centre myself and to control the underlying pain.

It is also important to note that overuse of the trigger does make it less effective over time, so it would need to be reactivated with the same exercise, using different anchors for different emotional states.

You can also use anchors with your partner to trigger feelings of pleasure in your intimate moments by utilising the same process. At the peak of emotional pleasure, use an anchor on your partner like rubbing their ear lobe in a certain way. This anchor can then elicit the same (but less intense, fortunately) feelings of pleasure when rubbing their same ear lobe in the same way at other times. The feelings of pleasure and affection will be reactivated and all will have a good time. Also, this powerful tool of affection will not be understood by anyone else, but it will be sure to get the attention of your partner. Quite a powerful little trick!

Using a mentor for guidance

Some people have knee-jerk, negative reactions to difficult situations and struggle to find better ways to respond. If you are struggling with finding the best way to deal with a negative situation, one option is to think about someone that you admire or someone who is skilled at resolving problems in a positive manner. This person becomes your "mentor" and they could be real or imagined a spiritual leader or an actor. You might also have different mentors for different situations.

There may be one in your favourite sport, one in your work situations and one in your personal life.

Some people may find it useful to use Jesus as a mentor, and ask the "WWJD?" question – "What would Jesus do?" For others it might be Gandhi, Clint Eastwood, James Bond, your parents, your teachers or any successful person in your desired field of sport or business. It doesn't matter who the mentor is, as long as it gets you on track for the best response and allows you to mirror high-level actions.

How Do You Create Great Life Habits?

Put this mentor into the situation that you are trying to handle and work through how you think that person would talk, act and feel through the process and how they would resolve the problem. You need to consider the type of words used and the tone of their voice, the fine details of their mannerisms and also how they make the other person feel through the process. Having created in your mind clear details of the whole event, you are then able to mirror these actions, words and feelings.

The first few times you do this for each situation, you will again have to "fake it until you make it" – acting and artificially creating the mannerisms. You will find it has the outcomes that you were looking for and repetition becomes easier. Before you know it, you will be behaving like this naturally and automatically and your new habit is in place.

This technique is especially useful if you find yourself repeatedly faced with a situation that you find annoying or emotionally draining, as there is something in that situation that is not being handled by you in a positive way. Now that you are 100% responsible for where you are at and how you feel, you now know that you need to find an alternative way to handle situations that make you feel like that. Examples would be the teenage kids shouting at you, the interview where you have to dismiss staff, or dealing with gossip.

A common example of this is when the senior staff or boss is away and a more junior person has to deal with a problem above their experience level. Imagining what the senior person would do and say to resolve the situation is likely to create a more successful result. Plus, this also reduces the pressure for the junior as they use their knowledge and skill of the senior to direct their actions.

So if you find yourself having difficulty dealing with a particular situation, think about what your positive mentor would do, work out the details and mirror it as closely as possible. The results should be just as good as if the mentors were doing it themselves. Problem solved!

Never judge

Over the years, we have each held many roles in both local and national organisations, as directors, chairman or board members, and in these roles we have had to deal with complaints of many types. Our experience has required us to deal with these in both professional as well as personal situations, and has dramatically brought home the importance of not jumping to conclusions, waiting to get all the information and not passing judgment until all the information is confirmed – rule number one of NITs!

It is always amazing how information and perception from one party can be so different from the other side. At first you hear one side of the story, and you think that this person has been severely mistreated in some way. Yet when the story from the other side is obtained, it is much less dramatic and often completely sensible. Usually the different views arise from a misunderstanding or lack of communication about the events that occurred.

Jane
A good example of this occurred at about 2am one Friday night at the emergency after-hours service, where Jane a 22-year-old lady arrived in a very confused state and unable to walk properly. Her mother was with her, as she had been called by her daughter when she was feeling unwell at a night club. Was she just drunk, had she taken any drugs, had she had her drink spiked, or was there some other medical problem going on? This was a potentially serious situation.

How Do You Create Great Life Habits?

In the doctor's eyes, he needed to get the girl to answer some very important questions and undergo a physical examination in order to assess what she could and could not do. Whenever he would ask the girl questions, the mother would step in and answer for her with "No, she doesn't take any drugs and wouldn't do that", and "Of course she has not too much to drink; she only ever drinks a few when she goes out." After repeatedly doing this, the doctor turned in frustration and said to the mother sternly, "I am asking your daughter and not you, so please let your daughter answer!"

Urgent investigations were organised and the patient was admitted and transferred to intensive care, but a letter of complaint from the mother followed. She said that the doctor had been rude and inconsiderate to a "young woman in distress", and that his manner was "inappropriate professionally" and "told me to shut up". Clearly the doctor could have been more diplomatic in the way he dealt with the mother, and a fuller explanation of why he wanted her to "shut up" would have gone down better. He was never rude or inappropriate, but the mother was extremely upset because of the situation and at the same time the doctor was extremely worried about the patient. High levels of stress on all sides and people having completely different agendas are a sure recipe for fireworks. Explanations were provided to the mother, with acknowledgement from the doctor that a fuller explanation would have been better, and all was resolved amicably.

An important aspect of these situations is that both parties are telling you different stories – but neither is lying. They are both telling you the truth as it appears to them, so in dealing with any situation, one person isn't necessarily correct and the other a liar. This simple realisation can overcome huge arguments with blame and recrimination as both parties learn the viewpoint of the other – hopefully!

If you prejudge a situation and make presumptions about one side or the other before both sides of the story is heard, you will falsely judge and draw incorrect conclusions. If the mother had been told "Of course he was wrong to tell you to shut up" before getting the full details, the situation would have aggravated unnecessarily. The risk would be that the person involved might use false justification to take further legal action based on only half the information. The situation is exactly the same with gossip, as you only have half of the information and this will often be distorted.

> The fundamental law of the Buddhists holds well here: "Never judge".

Attitude of gratitude

> Whole books have been written on this subject, and the underlying principle is that we need to be grateful and recognise the wonderful things that happen to us every day. This reinforces the positive events in our lives and focuses our minds on what is wonderful and great and takes the focus away from the negative challenges that we face.

This shifts your thinking and your emotions away from what is negative and draining, to what is good, uplifting and inspiring. The unresolved challenges in life will still need to be addressed, but set aside specific time to work on those issues and after that move your focus back to the wonderful things in your life. The tendency to dwell repeatedly on the negative unresolved problems in your life can drag you down because of the negative focus and not seeing the everyday wonders that you do have.

We can always find something to complain about if we allow the NITs to be our focus, but this will just attract more of the same bad stuff over time. Finding and searching for the positives in a situation is the fundamental aspect of the "Attitude of Gratitude," and goes hand in hand with developing a NIT-free life and environment.

Gratitude exercise

Before going to sleep every night, think of three things that you can be thankful for or experiences that went well that day. Consider new skills that you have learned, generous or altruistic acts that you have done or compliments that you have received from others. It is also important to enjoy the victories that you have had and when projects or difficult tasks are completed.

By thinking about three great things that happened each day, you reinforce your positive attitude and keep the great and wonderful things in front of you. This has a profound effect on your physiology, releasing the feel good hormones and stimulating your amygdala. Those great thoughts should also give you better quality sleep and you are likely to have better dreams too!

Summary

Strategies for changing previously entrenched habits like NITs require persistence, dedication and the use of various other techniques to lock in your newfound habits. Affirmations with intense emotional attachment develop and reinforce the positive approach and expectation in life in your subconscious.

Surround yourself with and generate laughter whenever you can, as this is great for your feelings of well-being as well as your health. Use mentors to mirror your behaviour when faced with difficult situations, never judge and always live with the "attitude of gratitude," being thankful for the wonders that life has provided for you. The technique of using anchors to immediately give you strength, commitment or stress reduction can be used at any time with great effects.

8

What About Our Children - The Next Generation?

> "Everybody knows how to raise children,
> except the people who have them."
> **P. J. O'Rourke**

Imagine a generation free of bullying, criticism, teasing and ganging-up, prejudice and with acceptance of all cultures, beliefs and differences. Instead of our children being subjected to bullying because of differences, they would be embraced and praised for their uniqueness. The world would become a phenomenally better place to live in. If we could move everyone towards this NIT-free state of mind, many of the major problems we face today would cease to exist!

While some would feel that the above statement seems far-fetched, we have had the privilege of experiencing this approach to life first hand. Ironically, these great attitudes came from the third-world countries and they can teach the developed nations great lessons on how to behave and the best way to bring up children!

Elizabeth: In each of the several trips to the South Pacific islands providing aid work, the attitude of the children towards each other was like a breath of fresh air. It was our own children who noticed it first. What they saw when they played with other kids in the park was that children of all ages were playing together and enjoying each other's company and skill levels without any fighting, bickering or unkind words. Even more surprisingly, included in the groups would be children with various disabilities or physical deformities from polio or cerebral malaria, albinos, cleft lips, and reduced IQ with Downs Syndrome children and other brain injuries.

The thing that was so lovely was that they were all playing together, the older and stronger ones giving the younger or disabled ones a fair play and at no time did anyone argue, fight or do or say nasty things to each other. If someone got hurt, they would all rush over to help and comfort the child. That was the best example of NIT-free children that we have ever experienced directly. They were also very quick and completely non-judgmental in playing with our children without any reluctance and despite the lack of a common language. It was so noticeably different from our "developed country's" playgrounds that our sons noticed it on their first visit and pointed it out to us right away!

So, we believe that this really is achievable for our future generations, our children's grandchildren and all who will inherit this planet. It is possible to develop a world where bullying and teasing are eliminated. We can enjoy all of our differences and uniqueness and be generous with our praise and support of everyone else around us.

How is this possible? How do we change a habit that has for generations been ingrained and accepted in our society? We believe that it starts with each one of us. Every one that inhabits the planet now is responsible for changing the world into a better place. We are talking about all of us: you, every parent, every teacher, siblings, friends, associates, and work colleagues. The grand "we" that is all of us; need to be the ones to move things in the right direction for a better future for our children, grandchildren and great grandchildren. We need to take action and not wait for others to do it - the time is now.

What About Our Children - The Next Generation?

> The beauty of dealing with the next generation is that it is a like a blank canvas where we can teach better ways of living and learning from our own past mistakes. We do need to action this across the whole population, but the exciting thing about children and adolescents is that the changes made now become the status quo in twenty years time.

Habits can be changed that previously would have seemed impossible! A good example from Australia is how the younger generation is now educated to be sun-smart and use sun block, hats and sunglasses. It is cool and trendy to be pale skinned, while the older generation is still struggling to let go of the "brown is beautiful" attitude that is associated with the world's highest skin cancer rates and wrinkly skin. So aiming for a NIT-free future generation is possible by teaching our children to live NIT-free lives.

Children learn what they live, therefore as parents, we need to be teaching our next generation the best principles. This must be done by example. We need to be living the principle, not just giving it lip service. We know that when a child is exposed to an environment of love, compassion and understanding, they respond to others in that way. The same is true for those unfortunate children who are subjected to a childhood of criticism, abuse, judgment and anger and adopt a negative, jaded perception of other people and the world.

Qualifications and training required for everything - Except your most important job in life!

Interestingly, society in developed countries has become obsessed with being trained correctly in our professions, trades and all jobs, taking optimal care in all forms of safety, correct protocols and work to ensure a safe and protected environment. However, regarding parenting, there is still no manual or guidelines for raising happy, healthy children that are positive and balanced. Nor is there a manual for creating an emotionally safe, supported and encouraging environment.

Being a parent is by no means an easy task and you only see the fruits of your labour after the children leave home and start their independent lives. Only at this time do you start to get a reprieve from the parenting role and the years of constant disciplining or frustration can create situations where the parents are frustrated or short tempered. This can result in NITs being thrown around and becoming well established in the lives of this new generation, who will then go and spread that approach to their children. So let's get this cycle to stop by eliminating NITs from our children's lives in this generation!

The most common emotion parents face is frustration, and from this emotion NITs breed furiously. Many times we have witnessed a parent so emotionally upset at their child's misbehaviour that the true message of what the right and wrong action is doesn't even get through to the child. In time, the parent wonders why this child is doing it again, and thinks the child is either stupid or insubordinate, when in reality the parent has failed to teach the child the lesson that was needed the first time round.

An example of this is when the child – say a teenager – misbehaves by shouting, being rude or saying inappropriate things to the parent. The common response from the parent is to shout back in order to be heard over the top of the shouting teenager. What is the child learning? They are learning that it is OK to shout, that it is quite acceptable to lose self-control and possibly even add in a few choice swear words back to you if these were used by you in the argument.

Frustration and impatience provides a fertile breeding ground for NITs, and because the child-rearing process goes on for a long time, if the NITs are not recognised and removed early, they become entrenched and become the status quo in your family and in the child's mind. Your efforts to "train" your

What About Our Children - The Next Generation?

children are therefore leading to them learning to use NITs, which is the opposite effect to what you are trying to achieve: happy, healthy, well-balanced and NIT-free children.

Children will require ongoing guidance until they leave the nest, so avoiding the negative emotions of frustration and impatience is important. As the parent, if you change these feelings to persistence, acceptance and patience (hopefully with inner peace), you will find you pass through the various stages of parenthood with less difficulty. Note, that challenges, worries and hurdles will still occur, but it is truly rewarding when your difficult or unruly teenager becomes a civilised, respectful adult and you start seeing the fruits of your efforts.

Let's look at some of the common NITs *(Table 3)* that are often thrown around at young and impressionable children. Remember that as the child's role model, you as the parent or teacher are the person that they trust and are learning from. So your words are more powerful and influential than anyone else's – you must choose your words wisely.

Mastering Negative Impulsive Thoughts (NITs)

Table 3. NITs in Children

NITs commonly used to children	NIT-free alternatives
I have told you a thousand times. You must be stupid!	What part of this are you struggling to understand? Or - You are very clever, so I know you will be able to do this properly. It just may take some practice and do your best.
You aren't as smart as your brother.	You are very clever and just need to practise this more (different from your brother).
This is all your fault.	Next time you will know what to avoid so you won't do it again.
You're a very bad boy/girl.	That's not the way a good boy/girl like you should act. We know you are a very good boy/girl and are surprised that you have acted in this way.
You are not allowed to do that	You are a very clever child so I would not expect you to behave in this way. I have told you this many times before because it is really important for your safety that you… We love you so much and don't want you to get hurt.

These are all very detrimental NITs, as they are telling the child that they are stupid, bad, at fault or deficient in some way, reinforcing that as a "bad child" they will continue to do bad things. What else would you expect within the child's mind than to believe what you have just told them?

What About Our Children - The Next Generation?

Here are some good strategies to follow in the highly charged situation of out-of-control children or teenagers:

- Don't react. Respond.

(We have said this before in Chapter 6, but it is very important with children!) Reactions come from an emotional base and will usually be personally judgmental and demeaning. Responses come from a values base where the problem is defined and the desired outcome is the focus. This takes the person out of the problem and focuses on the value-based qualities that will not be disputed (usually).

- Deep Breaths.

Take a few deep breaths, as this will give you time to think. Work out exactly what the message is that you want the child to get – be clear, to the point and positively reinforcing (NIT-free). Only say something once you have controlled your negative emotion and are able to deal with the child without anger or frustration, even if this is in ten or twenty minutes' time, or even two hours' time. You are allowed to say "Let's talk about this in an hour's time".

- Work out your message.

Formulate what you want to say in your own mind clearly before you say it, and make sure that the right message is clear in the words that you speak. You have to be in control of your own emotions in this process so that the child understands the message and is not just seeing your anger. It is also important to understand that while the child is out of control themselves, they are not in the right frame of mind to absorb any information anyway, so trying to ram your message down their throat will be doomed to failure. You will have to wait until the child has settled enough to listen and hear what you have to say before going into your speech. The child will learn much more quickly, when the adult gets the clear message across and they can both move on after the event with no anger, frustration or residual guilt.

All of the techniques that were described in dealing with third-party NITs apply to NITs that come from your beloved children:

- Avoid emotional involvement.
- Count to ten; bite your tongue if necessary.
- Remember that what your child says is the truth for them at the time.
- Wait for them to finish.
- Ask if they have missed anything.
- Remain empathetic and avoid judgment.
- Keep your integrity and keep calm, because this is exactly the sort of behaviour that you want them to mirror down the track.
- Trying to "walk in their shoes" to work out where they are coming from will also help.

With small children who are throwing a tantrum, you can use the counting downwards from five or ten to zero to give them a chance to settle down or stop the behavior. However with older children and teenagers, time out until you have both calmed down is probably better. The key here is more about the manner and respect you give them, so that they will give you that respect back – although it may take a few years.

Another important principle that all parents need to remember is that your role is to teach your children to be independent and balanced adults. Your whole purpose is to teach the children to not need you. Your role is therefore to teach the children to manage things for themselves, cook, clean, drive and make their own life decisions. The point here is that you need to let go and allow them to do things for themselves. If you are completely overbearing and controlling, without giving them the safe environment to make mistakes, they are more likely to make mistakes in an unsafe environment with more serious consequences.

Therefore, your role as a parent is to make yourself obsolete, and as the young adult starts flying independently away from home, you have to congratulate yourself on a job well done - hopefully. Just be there if they need any further advice and are willing to get it from you. It is all part of the rich tapestry of life.

NITs with teachers and sports coaches

Our beautiful children are impressionable and naïve and they will learn and take on whatever their environment shows them is the reality. It is unfortunate that some teachers and sports coaches, while motivated by good intent, are hopelessly deficient in the skill of positive encouragement and NIT-free teaching. A good exercise to do, if it is possible, is attend the coaching or teaching sessions to observe the atmosphere and attitudes of the teachers that are going to have a large influence over your children's minds. Is the approach a positive and supportive one that encourages the best out of your child, or is it aggressively derogatory, using negativity and fear to scare your children into performing better? Is it the carrot or the stick?

If the team loses, is everyone reprimanded as if this loss has created a world crisis? Are they only being told what they did wrong, or are their great efforts that were made given appropriate congratulations? Are they all involved in the sport for the fun and love of it, or are they all there purely to win at any cost? Do they congratulate the opposing team for a great performance, or are they teaching bad sportsmanship and poor behaviours?

Ask your Three Magic Questions about the words and actions from the coaches and it should be clear if they fall into the NIT category.

Evidence is clear that young people who are encouraged with negativity and fear will not continue to perform or participate in those sports and will choose to drop out in the longer term. This can happen with high-performing sports people where extremely high-level talents were just dropped because the constant negativity made them think that they weren't any good. Obviously in the academic arena, overbearing teachers with derogatory comments at students' efforts will demoralise them. As a result they will have the expectation that they will fail in the future – and as we now know, if that is what they believe, they will! NITs influence both the academic and the sports performance areas. You need to decide what teachers and attitudes you allow your child to be influenced by.

We were fortunate to have our children attend a school that based all their principles on support and love for each other, and were much less focused on results at any cost. It is clear that the influences of many hours of school life do affect children's outlooks, so keep your NIT filters on high alert. If there are attitudes from teachers that could be improved in your schools, raise the subject and get the standards improved! Most teachers are trying their best, and some would not even realise the negative effects that they are causing as "teaching has always been done this way!"

Choose your children's friends wisely!

Even the most positive and supportive parents will have their children influenced by others during their formative years. The old saying that "you become like the people you associate with" holds true for children as they go through childhood and especially through the anarchy of teenage years. As a parent of a young baby, you are devoted and loving to your child and surround them with positivity and support. All may be going really well until at four or five years of age they go to various forms of kindergartens or pre-schools where they are exposed to the unfiltered attitudes of their peers.

What About Our Children - The Next Generation?

The attitudes and behaviours of the children they associate with and have as their friends at every level of schooling will rub off on them. The hard-working, motivated and high achievers will all spur each other on to higher performance. The lazy, negative and destructive attitudes of the rebel groups will usually end up as the smokers, drug users and school drop-outs. As a parent, therefore, while you can't choose who your child makes friends with, you can use your subtle influence to encourage more associations with their friends with better attitudes.

John: One of our sons was brought home by the police one afternoon at the age of thirteen, having been caught throwing water bombs at passing cars. Stupidly, he and his friend had not noticed that it was a police car that they were aiming at, so they were caught red-handed. Our son took full responsibility for it, saying that it was his idea and his fault, and that no harm was meant. He was openly apologetic to the police and his "suitably severe" parents in front of the police. After the police had gone, we asked him what that was all about. He admitted that he took the blame, even though it was not his idea, as his friend "would have been killed by his father" if he had admitted to being the culprit. Our son was just protecting his friend and therefore a minor reprimand from us on being more careful about what he was doing was all he got as punishment. We felt that his martyrdom to protect his friend was honourable and fortunately, he learnt his lesson and progressed through school and university without any further police incidents, so no harm done.

As a parent, paying attention to the attitudes and behaviours of the parents of your child's friends will give some clue as to the direction of their children and what your child will be exposed to in their house. In your quest for the best NIT-free environment for your children, encourage them to choose their friends and associates wisely

Social media

We have mentioned a number of times in earlier chapters the power of TV and movies in affecting both your feeling of internal happiness as well as your attitudes. Similarly, if you or your child is spending a lot of time using their computer, mobile phones or any of the other electronic devices and being exposed to constant strong negative input, this will affect both their self-esteem, mood and life attitudes. There are many stories of school children being bullied, intimidated and tormented with these forms of communication, and the seriousness of the impact must not be underestimated. We have seen depression, complete loss of self-esteem and suicides as a result.

This has also been the case at universities and in organisations where the use of webcams and the easy and fast transmission into the online public domain. Personally sensitive information or images have been distributed and abused, breaching all normal, acceptable standards. Legal protections have been slow to keep up with the technology and social media, so there have been and still are huge legal gaps in this area.

However, in the social media and online realm, the first principles of NITs still hold true. By asking the Three Magic Questions, the underlying nature of NITs will be exposed. Then it is important to apply pressure to the individuals or organisations that carry the data to withdraw it using the principles of civilised behaviour, even if the legal boundaries are not yet in place.

As consumers, our power is with our feet, and threatening to boycott, or actually boycotting a service, is likely to have a significant impact. Always keep the NIT filters on high alert. Let's have the expectation that the providers of the social media services should be obligated to maintain the standards of an obviously NIT-free environment, and encourage or force them to filter or block the clearly malicious and NIT-based material.

Summary

As parents, teachers, coaches and lecturers, we are all holding the developing seeds of our future generations in our hands. The outcomes for the future generations will be determined by our actions. The responsibility is in our hands whether our children live their lives with mutual respect, positivity and supportiveness; or if they are negative, derogatory and critical of others. The key to having great results comes down to ensuring that the teaching that our children receive is free of NITs.

Understanding, recognising and removing NITs from your home, schools and universities will be the first step in keeping your children safe from NITs. Then giving them the skills to recognise and control NITs themselves will have positive effects for their future and everyone around them. Being aware of the different sources of these NITs, whether it is your children's friends, their parents, TV, movies or social media, will allow you to reduce the amount of negative influence that these impressionable youngsters will receive. When more parents, teachers, coaches and lecturers become aware of NITs and avoid them in their teaching, NITs will be eliminated from children's environments, and this will have massive benefits for the future generations. The effects will progressively flow across the whole world.

9

Negative Impulsive Thoughts In Intimate Relationships And Love

> "Life is not measured by the number of breaths we take, but by the number of times our breath is taken away!"
> **Anon**

It is interesting that the philosophy around karma is that you get back what you give out. In other words, you need to give out the sorts of things that you want back. Therefore if you want love, you need to give out love; if you want happiness, you need to give out happiness.

> The first key to personal happiness and love is that it is essential that you have happiness and love within yourself; otherwise you have none to give away.

It certainly seems to be the case that if you do not have this internal happiness and self-love established, it is much harder to form deep and rewarding relationships with others, because the tendency is that you use your relationship to replace your own deficiencies. Obviously everyone has different areas of strength, and most strong relationships benefit from the other person's strengths and vice versa. But if this is not in a balanced way and for mutual benefit, problems tend to arise within the relationship.

The second key is being able to share your own internal happiness and love with others, and the most important second person here is your partner. Having a strong, intensely rewarding intimate relationship seems to be the thing that makes us all feel complete - a pleasure shared seems to be a pleasure doubled! Looking at a beautiful sunset or view always seems more wonderful when it is shared, and amazing experiences in life seem more special when you can share them with someone you care for.

The most fundamental principle of life is that what we all want most in life is to be loved! This principle is unrelated to age or culture, because from childhood to old age, being loved is the most desired emotion and it crosses cultural boundaries. The power of love becomes evident when it is taken away, whether by physical separation, emotional separation, death or divorce. Emotional devastation often follows. Some people try to get love with money, power, threats or self-deprivation but for a successful relationship it needs to be balanced with both sides benefitting equally. One-sided relationships where the giving and taking is out of balance results in problems. The most successful and sustainable relationships, in personal and business life, are based on balance and fairness using the win-win principle.

So, for each of us to be truly and deeply loved, we need to have enough love for ourselves and enough self-acceptance that we feel worthy of being loved. When anyone feels that they are unworthy of the deep and intense love that they are receiving from another person, they will reject it and sabotage the relationship. This will pop up in the relationship in many ways, from direct verbal doubting of their worthiness to more subtle activities that undermine or possibly destroy the relationship completely. This is the subconscious creating the future that it expects, and it is all based on NITs. The key here is to ensure that you have enough self-love and self-acceptance to believe that you are worthy of this wonderful love or this wonderful person, and gratefully accept their love and adoration.

Talking about self-love and self-acceptance here is not in the arrogant sense that "I am the best" or "Everyone will love me because I am so good." It is more along the lines of "I am a worthy, decent and a good person who deserves to find ultimate love and affection from the one person ideally suited to me." This is not in any way putting yourself above or superior to anyone else. The self-acceptance is about accepting yourself as you are with all your great strengths and areas of weakness. Although certain areas may not be perfect, you have a plan for the things you want to change and the things you are happy to leave alone. This is all about avoiding NITs in your attitude to yourself, accepting your weaknesses and allowing yourself to be loved – because if you can't love yourself, you will never let anyone else love you either!

As we saw with Clive in Chapter 2, self doubt and personal NITs can sabotage your self esteem and destroy your marriage and relationships.

So here we are in the chapter about relationships, talking about your personal NITs again – interesting isn't it? They are showing themselves to be important little critters, aren't they? It all comes back to the importance of having a good attitude to yourself and good expectations to allow good outcomes to follow. NITs can undermine it all. Having self-love and self-appreciation is also necessary to be a well-rounded and complete human being who is so much more likely to attract your ideal partner.

If you are looking for a partner and finding it hard to find "the one", work on being the best that you can be, and that wonderful person that you are will attract "the one" for you! You are only likely to do that if you, your thoughts and your actions are free of NITs.

Achieving the ultimate relationship!

Given that so much of our happiness relies on finding and developing the ultimate relationship, we do want to give it the space it deserves. If you want to have a perfect relationship, you will need to have a relationship that is free of NITs although being free of NITs alone is not enough. You will need the relationship to have the opposite of NITs – lots of Positive Affirmative Thoughts (PATs) produced and shared for both yourself and for your partner.

In the ultimate relationship, both parties give themselves unconditionally without keeping tabs or a scorecard on who has given more. Both sides give generously and in a balanced manner, depending on each side's needs at the time. There will be times when one is under the hammer and needing extra help, and at other times the tables will be turned. Each gets the support that they need when they need it – "what you lose on the swings, you gain on the roundabouts!" This is all done freely and without conditions or feelings of indebtedness.

Both sides will be supportive of the other party, emotionally and practically, no matter what the other person is going through at that time. For example, if one of you has to work extended hours, you understand that your partner would prefer to spend time with you and will work as fast and hard as possible to get home as soon as they can.

Regardless of where you both are, when you are apart you know you would rather be together – keep holding that thought and have the attitude of gratitude for the wonderful relationship that you do have. Use that power to help you through the times of separation, as it can seem like an eternity.

To cement the ultimate relationship you must both have no doubt about each other's commitment to the relationship.

Negative Impulsive Thoughts In Intimate Relationships And Love

This is developed by complete and absolute honesty to each other about what you want in life. If you don't want to be with each other, then be honest about that too and go your separate ways. Living a lie is doomed and likely to end up the same way anyway – just with more regrets and hurt feelings. This will also eliminate the jealousy that is obviously one of the biggest and baddest NITs around! Speak openly, be honest, maintain the attitude of gratitude and flip any jealous thoughts into PATs.

One of the interesting features of wonderful relationships is that in these situations, each person puts more value on their partner's happiness than their own. It is out of this altruistic desire to fulfill your partner's needs that you can get immense joy. The wonderful thing is that in this ideal relationship, your partner is doing the same thing for you, so it is bells and whistles all around. Taking the focus away from your own needs and without expectation, putting your efforts into making your partner happy changes the whole focus and emphasis of what you do. Your attentiveness, awareness and sensitivity are dramatically increased. This is very noticeable for your very grateful and fulfilled partner, who will be looking to share that feeling back with you and give you just the same adoration and love back. Swings and roundabouts again.

Laugh with your partner every day and fill your relationship with joy. Don't take yourself too seriously and find humour in the small things in life. Give your partner sincere compliments frequently, not just when you want something.

If you like the way they look, say it! If you can see their silhouette and it is sexy, make the comment. If you feel like kissing them, hugging them or making love to them and the circumstances are not suitable, let them know that they do it for you! This will create the situation that you are making each other feel good every day, without ulterior motive, and that gives it more value.

Let them know how proud you are of them and their achievements, and receive compliments with gratitude and acceptance. Tell them why you love them and how wonderful they make you feel when they do thoughtful things for you.

Complimenting each other and focusing on what is right with each other helps you focus on what is right and not what is wrong. This builds up each other's self-acceptance and self-love, resulting in the cementing of the foundations of your relationship. When two whole, self-fulfilled people come together, ready to give 100% to the relationship, the outcomes are fantastic.

Be open with your affection and compliment each other in public – "Here comes my beautiful wife/husband/partner" – touch them gently and affectionately, and hold their hands. This affectionate approach to each other is contagious, and soon everyone around starts to do the same thing! This mutual affection also deters predators who might want to try their luck with your partner, but as your relationship is so secure, this is a non-issue anyway. The relationship will never fall apart, because you love each other too much and it is balanced and mutually rewarding.

Showing respect to each other is another key, as not showing respect erodes the foundations of the relationship and each other. An example is to ask your partner for confirmation of plans if you are invited out as well as discussing important decisions with them. While you may know what the answer will be, it is courteous and respectful to confirm it with them. This will also confirm that your expectations were correct.

Most people would like their relationship to stay in the honeymoon period, when everything was fresh and exciting. Well you can, but it is up to you! If that is what you want, you need to treat your relationship as if it is still in that honeymoon period – continue to take care, pay attention to what your partner says and wants, buy her (or him) flowers, do nice touches, make things special, show that you care and the excitement can persist for years and years!

Know your partner and pay attention – what they like to do, their favourite foods, TV, music, colour, places to visit, who is their favourite mentor, what gives them the most pleasure (sexual and non-sexual). Make an effort to make the things that are important to your partner important to you, so even though you don't really like football, try and get involved, and even if you don't understand why she likes flowers, just buy them!

You should know these things, because if you are going to make them happy, you need to know what works for them. People do feel loved when you pay attention to the finer details. Be able to comfort your partner and help each other emotionally and practically to solve any problems by working together – "What do we have to do to solve this?" or "How can I help you so we get through this?" Work as a team and use the terms like "we", "us" and "together" to emphasise the team effort. Know each other's strengths and weaknesses – praise them for one and help them with the other.

Obviously, both of you are going to need to know about NITs, but when you look at your relationship and communication, are the things that you say to each other mostly positive and uplifting or mostly critical and negative? Once aware of the principle, you can recognise the NITs and start eliminating them and approaching things from the other side with so much better results!

Sometimes you might need to imagine what your partner is dealing with to understand why they are tired, irritable or home so late. Go through the exercise of "walking in their shoes for a day" by asking them in detail what they have to do. You may well find out why one person may need some quiet time when they get home, rather than immediately giving the children to the worker on their arrival home.

A good relationship is also one where you respect what the other person needs, even if that is actually taking some time for themselves (without you). A secure and complete relationship will have the security of knowing that they do want to be together and will rejoin with a renewed appreciation after the time has passed.

Communication in relationships is critical too. Use honest and simple language, without any double meanings or innuendos, making sure that what you say is exactly what you mean. Everything you say should be taken at face value, so if something is upsetting you, say what it is, and don't talk around the subject. If you are asked if you want to do something or not, be honest – for example "Well, I am very tired and would prefer not to go, but it is important for you so I am happy to come to support you".

Make sure there is no hidden indebtedness and be honest. If one partner only does things to create a "debt" from the other person, this undermines the positive energy of the relationship severely. The result is then both sides have to do things because they need to and not because they want to. Do what you do because you love your partner and allow your partner to not do what they don't want to do because you love them too. As long as the balance is present, this works well.

Constant sarcasm, guilt and innuendo with implications of criticism or ungratefulness leaves the other person constantly trying to work out what they are doing wrong. This undermines the relationship and if that approach continues, the person will often either pull back from their partner or withdraw from the relationship completely.

Honesty sometimes requires you to be courageous, and both parties also need to be strong enough to hear the truth without being offended. Once the truth is out and the main issues are clear, you can then work together to solve the problems. But at least you are focused on the real problem, not the underlying excuses that circulate when the truth is too hard to discuss.

Remember that we all change and grow over the years, so the nature of someone that you met aged twenty may not be what they are like at thirty or fifty! Don't assume that you know them – ask them and listen attentively so you keep up to speed with any changing aspects of their desires, dreams and plans, as your plans ideally are going in the same direction.

> Having a great relationship in a NIT-free environment is also great for your children, as they learn from it all and will tend to mimic your actions and behaviours.

Fill the Emotional Bank for ultimate rewards!

Understanding the different responses and needs of men and women to love, affection and sex, does give us the answers on how to make everyone phenomenally happy. The ultimate answer to what women want and how to deal with men is right here! Remembering that while we all want to be loved, men and women have different needs.

Women are emotional beings who feel the love with their emotions first. This builds with the affection, attention and pampering given by their partner. It is emotional foreplay that creates the momentum of desire, with the ultimate outcome of love-making when the emotional love banks are full and overflowing.

> Sex is therefore the by-product of emotional fulfillment and not usually a purely physical desire from the woman's side.

Men, on the other hand, have more emphasis on their physical desires, and the emotional love bank is a nice addition that adds (very dramatically sometimes) to the primary physical pleasure. Woman can view this very physical desire as non-specific and therefore not directed at them personally. They can sometimes take the view that this desire is not "love" but lust and can be equally fulfilled by any other woman. While this may or may not be the case, the man will need to build up the woman's emotional bank to the point where she feels filled with love and affection towards him and then happy endings result. One of the important points here is that the woman's emotional bank can be worked on at any time and definitely should not be just before sexual advances are made.

For example, the tokens of love and affection that work so well for the woman can be repeated little compliments of how gorgeous she is, how much you love her, little touches and strokes, offering her assistance when she doesn't expect it, looking adoringly into her eyes, buying her flowers, chocolates, bringing her treats in bed or leaving a flower on her pillow. You can even start topping up her love bank immediately after the sexual act with ongoing affection, caressing, talking and tenderness that will all add up to her being full of love and affection sooner – this is often a time of increased appreciation of the affection so probably earns you double points: win-win!

From the woman's perspective, she really wants the love and affection, and the physical act is often a secondary result. However, if she wants to get more love and affection from her man, the easiest way is to take charge of the sexual advancement and be the one to pursue him and surprise him with unsolicited sex and give him what he is looking for. He is then sexually fulfilled and being pursued, taking the pressure off him to make all the advances! By changing the dynamics in this way, he is more likely to give the woman the compliments and affection that she desires. This also takes the pressure off the woman as she now is more in control of the events and can make the timing suit herself! This also avoids the need to turn him down and avoids the flow on self doubt and negative feelings in him.

Obviously, the woman would have to go through with the act a few times and give him what he is looking for, but this is at times when she feels like it. It also puts spark back in the relationship when the woman does the pursuing and the man then does feel the love and feels desirable, so this whole process will have surprisingly good outcomes!

NITs in separation and divorce

Having just been releasing all your feel-good hormones with thoughts of having the ultimate relationship, we will now discuss the opposite! In relationship breakdowns, separations and divorces, people are faced with major life changes and self-doubt. It is like having your whole life thrown up in the air with loss of established life habits and the status quo. Then the two people have to wait to see how all the pieces of their lives settle back down again over time with only some of these pieces being able to be controlled.

Unfortunately, there will always be negative thoughts about themselves and about their ex-partner, and these NITs are usually thrown around at each other and often to all their children, relations, friends, work colleagues and even strangers.

Separations and divorces are possibly the source of the strongest and most destructive NITs, because they are coming from someone who knows all your innermost fears and insecurities, your sensitive heart strings and your personal loves and hates. No-one will escape experiencing some NITs in this situation, so be prepared: make sure you recognise them as they are forming in your mind and from your ex-partner so you need to neutralise and destroy them fast! This is possible, and as you get better at the process, it will make your life through these hard times much less unpleasant.

Any vicious and denigrating NITs from an ex-partner at this time can be understood, at least to some extent, as they are hurt

Mastering Negative Impulsive Thoughts (NITs)

or upset and just trying to hurt you back. They may even try to influence everyone else in your social circles to take sides or affect the children. As time passes in the separation, the strong and negative emotions will wane and people will ease off the vitriol and hopefully everyone will get on with their new lives. Some people take longer than others, but it is important to protect yourself from the NITs during this time.

In the heat of separations and divorces there seems to be a fairly classic pattern of accusations that fly from one party to the other, achieving the "extreme NIT" classification. You must understand that these NITs are usually deliberate attempts to denigrate you, damage your reputation and/or your self-worth.

So the usual pattern is as follows, although the order may vary:

- "You will never find anyone who will love you as much as I did."
- "You have had an affair/gratuitous sex/orgies."
- "You have taken all the money and left me penniless."
- "I am going to take all the money and ruin you."
- "You were useless in bed and never gave me satisfaction."
- "You are deserting the kids."
- "The kids will never speak to you again."
- "Your reputation at work will be ruined."

When you analyze the pattern, they are attacking you in every area of your life from your self-worth to your relationship, sexual, parenting and professional skills. Thrown in are likely to be accusations of you having an affair, being a thief, liar and a scoundrel and probably some financial accusations as well. This interestingly covers all the value systems, so be prepared to have every one attacked if your ex-partner is falling into this NIT-producing behaviour.

Unfortunately, the NITs may become more targeted and personally vindictive as time goes on, or where your ex is feeling that they are not getting what they want. For example:

- "I will take you to the cleaners." (Financial threat)
- "I will never let the kids see you again." (Parental threat)
- "I will ruin your reputation at work and in the community." (Professional threat)
- "At least I am having sex with someone that can give me pleasure!" (Personal denigration).

And so it goes on...

For the protection of your heart, your happiness and your balance, you must recognise all these NITs and identify your sensitive areas. You can think of the process as your ex-partner having hooks in your heart and they will regularly twist them, jerk them or use them to try and pull you back into the relationship or just back into an argument. For some, even though there may be no hope of reconciliation, they may well use the hooks (kids, money, divorce legalities, maintenance costs, and your values) just to have some contact with you, because for many people who have been left – the "dumpees" – they may not yet have come to terms with the separation.

The person who actively chooses to leave the relationship – the "dumper" – would usually have gone through their entire emotional trauma before making the decision to leave the relationship. For this reason they have already come to terms with the separation and now just want to move on. This difference in perception allows the dumper to understand why the dumpee "never seems to be able to move on".

It is often the case, though, that the dumper and dumpee will usually both be actively involved in NIT propagation, whether it is personally in their own heads or verbally to the ex-partner and others around. Never think that you may be immune from NITs, as you will have your own and have to deal with many from your ex! Also understand that you are in a highly infective state as your resistance and immunity is down, having been through the trauma of separation.

Step 1 – Recognise the NITs from both sides.

As with all NITs, the first key in the separation and divorce situation is to recognise them forming in your mind and recognise the ones being sent to you from the ex – directly or through children, friends, relations and strangers. If the statements are not supportive, helpful or empowering, then they are NITs and need to be treated with Stop, Drop and Roll. Practise letting them flow away like water off a duck's back or like something you are witnessing blowing past in the wind. Alternatively, practise wrapping them up with love and sending them back with compassion and understanding, as that person has some growth to experience!

Step 2 – Recognise your weaknesses and the hooks.

The second key is to recognise all those sensitive and important areas in your makeup that your ex-beloved is targeting with hooks and line to draw you back in. These are commonly personal denigration, children issues, behavioural issues (their's, your's or the kids') and money issues. These hooks need to be individually recognised and removed from your emotional psyche one by one. Think of the lines that attach the hooks being cut and the hooks being physically removed from your body. Remember that the struggle will go on, as the other party will send out more of the same hooks or target other areas of your life if one area doesn't seem to be affecting you.

Once you recognise the hooks and lines that are attaching you to the ex and start removing them, you will feel an amazing liberation and lightening of your emotional load. The ex will recognise when they are not getting the reactions from you that they expect, and without you saying anything about it, they will know when certain hooks are not working.

You will know when you have taken your power back, because you can feel it and so can they – and they will not be happy about it. They will throw out more vigorous, vindictive and unpleasant hooks before they eventually give up, but this may take years. As their comments become more and more extreme, they have to stretch the truth further and further and it does become clearer to all parties, including your children, that what is being said is not the reality and only coming from the aggrieved dumpee.

As mentioned regularly, "What goes around comes around." We develop our own karma from the actions we take and whatever we put out we will get back, often multiplied many times. Sometimes it takes a long time to occur, and the best approach is to have compassion and sympathy for the person who is behaving like that and for the future suffering that the person will experience as a result. Your job is to focus on how you feel, keep your internal balance and harmony, maintain a class act, return the bad stuff with your love and do not worry about things that seem overwhelming – in a few years, they will be insignificant!

Expanding on the insignificance of seemingly monumental issues, there are good examples of people who have lost "all of their money" in a separation but bounced back to make much more much faster after that. Eventually the children grow out of being affected by the denigration coming from the other party and recognise that the denigrator is the one at fault.

In the early stages of you having to deal with targeted or malicious NITs, make sure that your ex-beloved gets no hint that their comments are having any effect on you at all even if they are. Like any schoolyard bully, they only continue if they think that they are affecting you, so "Fake it until you make it!" Keep your cool and let their comments be a reflection of their low-level functioning and have no bearing on you.

To maintain your power and strength and to reduce the power of the NIT producer, you need to respond to all the NITs with indifference, acceptance and love. When the person starts to see no reaction from you and gets the feeling that you don't care what they do anymore, they are likely to start to behave normally and not just keep trying to hurt you.

> So the faster you can remain poker-faced, shrug your shoulders and not rise to the baits that are set for you, the faster they will return to behaving like the normal human beings they are.

Step 3 – Make a list.

The third important strategy is to develop a list of your desires in life that accurately reflect how you want to live in the future, how you want your relationships to work and what your future partner will be like. In relation to your partner, this needs to be very detailed with all aspects of the relationship covered from their physical appearance to their behaviour, attitude, communication, and how you will interact. Making this list will take several hours and days of thinking and working through the different areas, but it's really important to develop this clear vision of who you are, what you want and where you are going in life – and the more specific on each of the issues the better.

It is very similar to goal-setting, but in this situation, you need to focus and design how you want to live and what your future partner will be like with as much detail as possible. The key, though, is that it has to be written down.

Write it down in a safe place and keep referring to the list regularly, modifying it as you think of more things. It also gives you a very clear idea of what you want in life, and looking back, it is often the case that the list and lifestyle expectations that you want from your life partner cannot be fulfilled by your ex-partner. Perhaps if you had made that list earlier in life, you may have not got into the relationship to start with or got out of it faster. Having the specifics laid out attracts to you the sort of person that you are looking for and also allows you to clearly see when people pass you in everyday life if they fall into your ideal partner category.

The good news from the children's perspective in separation is that they are a lot more resilient than we give them credit for. Often situations that appear catastrophic at the time drift into insignificance over the years, and looking back, the children usually cope in a variety of ways, grow up eventually and then can see that the behaviour in the malicious parent was inappropriate. Having the strength to let things slide and having faith that time will allow resolution to most of these actions is very important. This is much the same as having the strength to walk away from situations, leaving karma to deal with the offending person, not embroiling yourself in the rights and wrongs of the issue and not becoming personally involved and part of the problem.

Other tools to deal with separation NITs:

Allowance – this incredibly important skill will improve your personal happiness and internal balance. This is the principle that you allow other people to think and behave as they want without any judgment or criticism. You will live your life as you think and believe is right and leave them to do the same, knowing that you cannot change the other person. They are functioning at whatever level they are at and you will allow them to be there without you having any judgment or negative emotion.

Allowance gives each person the freedom to have their own thoughts and beliefs and each person will reap the rewards that they deserve without criticism from others. In the event that you do not like the actions that person is maintaining, you need to live your life separately – which is exactly what you have just done! You have even less control of your ex now than when you were together, so don't even think that you might be able to change their behaviour – if you couldn't in the years of your relationship, then you won't make any difference now! Also now it is none of your business.

The second tool is love! Firstly love yourself, just as we discussed earlier, but it is more critical here in the "separation war zone." Remind yourself of all your positive features and wonderful aspects. Build up your self-confidence by going over your past successes in life, love, relationships, supportive comments made by friends and partners in the past and really find the great things that are in you. This self-love will protect you from all the levels of NITs and denigration that will be flying around in this traumatic but temporary time. Build up the intensity of your memories so that the positive emotions are overflowing in your heart and you are full of great feelings and emotions. Any time that you are attacked with personal NITs that erode your feelings, go back to your memories and relive those great times so you know they are possible for you to achieve again.

A good strategy to use when you recognise NITs being thrown at you is to observe them as external to your body and your emotions (i.e. holding them outside yourself) and just look at them. Imagining that you have a glass barrier or force field around you and you choose what comes in and what is kept outside gives you this control. Recognise the fact that they are NITs and have no right to be let into your emotions, wrap them up with love, just like the "box technique" and send them back to their sender or just let them float past. This way the NIT is not allowed into your emotional state and no further harm will come of the negative energy.

In most instances, no reaction is the best reaction, but if intervention is required, use the strategies described earlier for 3rd party NITs.

Abusive relationships and NITs

Abusive relationships are where NITs have been taken to extremes of denigration and undervaluing one person. Abuse usually arises from a prolonged period of NITs being used to undermine the person's self-confidence to the point where they feel worthless. This is done by repeatedly having very negative things said to them about how useless they are, how unattractive they are, and how poorly they perform in various ways, until the person believes these negative things.

When the abuser has achieved this, they are able to totally control the other person as that person feels and believes that they are so unattractive or worthless that no one else will love them. They even believe that they deserve to be treated in this way!

Recognising NITs early in this process will hopefully save many thousands of women (and men) from becoming entrenched in this pattern of behaviour. Early recognition will allow the comments to be disregarded, questioned or challenged at an early stage and prevent escalation. If already established, the strategies need to be firstly to protect yourself from the NITs, don't accept the statements as fact and certainly do not take them into your emotions.

Secondly, filter them out and only take on board the information that will give you strength and power. If it is not helpful and empowering, let it slide past your personal space like water off a duck's back or like leaves blowing past in the wind – they are of no consequence to you.

If you already have established, internalised and strongly developed NITs on board, these need to be progressively destroyed and removed. Use whichever visualisation or process that works for you to Stop, Drop and Roll the NITs, replacing them with good, healthy and positive beliefs about yourself, especially along the following lines:

- You deserve happiness and joy.
- You are a wonderful person with great qualities.
- You have a kind heart and enormous amount of love to share.
- You have worked hard and should reap the rewards.
- You want to be with someone who appreciates and loves you.

If necessary you may have to deal with these concepts:

- If he/she truly loved me, he/she wouldn't treat me badly.
- I would rather be alone and happy than together and abused.
- The children will be better off with us separated, or they will learn that the abusive behaviour is acceptable and do it themselves!

The most important thing to remember is that you need to control what is going on in your own mind, and filter out disempowering, unsupportive and unloving information. You are looking for love and happiness like everyone else, and while your partner can say the words "I love you" easily, the actions show the very different emotion of control and power. Also, if that is what their "love" is, do you really want it?

After all, it is still your choice to do with your life what you want, be with whom you want to be with and enjoy the things in life that you want. You can accept this behaviour if you wish, but never consider that you don't have a choice – the door is there for you to walk out, the sand is there to draw the line in, and the limits on what you will accept in life can be set at any moment.

Just drifting and accepting a deteriorating situation without thinking about what you are prepared to accept in life is your choice. Make that choice wisely and for your long-term good.

You do have control over your life, but clearly you made the decision to stay in that situation and allowed that person to behave in those ways. You allowed those NITs to be implanted in your brain and you accepted them as the truth. You still have the choice to reconsider all of those thoughts one by one and eliminate them from your mind, replacing them with useful and empowering thoughts that more accurately reflect your deeper truth.

Taking responsibility for being where you are in this kind of situation is extremely hard, but does give you the power to get out of it by taking back control over your life, your boundaries, your aspirations and dreams for the future.

Summary - for the Ultimate Wonderful Relationship

Imagine what it would be like to be in a relationship where you never argued, are always loving and kind to each other, always respectful, honest, sensitive and complimentary. Imagine having a mutually rewarding relationship with open communication, constant positivity, trusting, close, fulfilling and without agendas. Imagine giving and receiving amazing levels of physical and emotional pleasure to each other without any issues of power or control. Imagine knowing 100% that your love for each other is so strong that there would never be anyone or anything to come between you, and that however tough life was externally, that your relationship would be solid and indestructible.

It is possible – we know this! We have seen it in others and have experienced the wonder of it ourselves. We have experienced the irony of having the worst catastrophes of our lives occurring simultaneously with the most incredibly wonderful loving experiences. The amazing thing was that the love, peace and trust inside the relationship stayed solid while everything else in our world fell apart! Time heals, and the pieces of your life do come back together, but throughout this time, this great love and affection stayed with us – what a great feeling!

Don't settle for less than you deserve. Expect the best, do the right things and be clear about your expectations. If you are with the right person who loves and values you, the more you give, the more you will get back.

Summary - continued

Aim high and love generously – it is just as wonderful to give phenomenal pleasure, as it is to receive it!

We have now passed a decade since we first began our relationship and the upmost respect, adoration, passion and love still exists today as it did all those turbulent years ago. The interesting feeling is that our relationship still feels like it did in the honeymoon phase. This is a result of us both sacredly honoring each other and putting into practice what we have just shared in this chapter – it really works!

Imagine how wonderful it is when you keep giving generously, and as a result, you keep being rewarded with more and more of the great stuff in return! It really does work – but it is up to YOU!

10
Negative Impulsive Thoughts In The Workplace

> "The three great essentials to achieve anything worthwhile are first, hard work; second, stick-to-itiveness; third, common sense."
> **Thomas Edison**

Imagine a workplace where all staff members are supportive of each other, working together for the good of the clients, company and each other. There is no criticism, sarcasm, gossip, denigration or negative comments. Imagine how much more pleasant it would be going to work, how much more productive you would be. Plus your job satisfaction and wonderful workplace atmosphere would improve your interactions with clients and other staff and undoubtedly result in a more profitable business. This is clearly a win–win–win situation in every direction.

So is this utopia actually possible? Is this utopia worth working towards? If you work in a full-time job, you will be spending more of your waking hours in your workplace than any other single environment. Therefore it is really important that this part of your life is pleasurable, joyful and that it boosts your energy and vitality.

It is also really interesting that the atmosphere in every workplace is absolutely determined by the attitudes and behaviours of the workers in that space, and as a worker it is therefore within your control! Obviously to create a wonderful, happy, NIT-free work environment, it requires widespread cooperation amongst all staff to learn and agree to the principles. NIT recognition and treatments need to be learned and also skills to overcome problems in a positive manner. Techniques are needed to resolve negative situations and to prevent any problems from becoming personal or judgmental attacks on individuals.

The interesting reality that occurs in organisations that adopt the NIT-free policies is that everyone develops much more interpersonal respect, appreciation and empathy. The results are tangible in businesses that adopt these attitudes and it is much more pleasant working in a business where everyone has mutual respect for what they do. You will also find each staff member is thankful for everyone else in each of their particular roles, allowing the business to run smoothly. From the junior that fills the stationery to the cleaners that keep the toilets pleasant through to the top manager that makes high-level decisions, everyone is needed and everyone should be valued.

Support from the business owners or superiors in any workplace is critical as the workplace culture needs to be achieved throughout all levels of the business, but it can start from the bottom or the top. The benefits to business are obvious, recognisable and easy to adopt so it is a relatively easy concept to "sell" to senior management. Everyone will benefit as the productivity improves, work satisfaction and morale improves, outcomes and services to clients improve and staff retention will also benefit. Even more wonderful is the cost and risk is low and the potential benefits are immense!

Recognising workplace NITs

Just like when dealing with NITs in your personal life, the first step is to recognise NITs. NITs in the workplace will arise in the form of negative thoughts towards fellow workers, the supervisor or boss, clients, the job itself or new processes that are put in place. These take many forms and can be recognised as derogatory statements, personal attacks, sarcasm, gossip or general negativity. Examples of these include:

- "God, I hate this job."
- "I just can't wait for the end of the day."
- "We'll never be able to complete this contract on time."
- "The boss is only interested in money."
- "She is so manipulative/trashy/up herself/pompous/nasty, etc."
- "He/she is useless and doesn't pull his/her weight."
- "Have you heard that he/she is having an affair with…?"
- "I heard he/she was fired from her last job because…"

Just start to listen to the tone of the conversations in your workplace and you will begin to recognise the NITs that are almost certainly flying around. If your workplace is NIT-free, congratulations! You will be in the top few percent of businesses. To achieve that level, a significant effort would have been put in place with staff improvement and developing the positive culture that avoids negativity in staff behaviour. Educating staff in workplaces about NIT principles will assist all businesses, even those with good staff attitudes as these skills will reinforce the good processes already in place, and be an extra tool that improves workplace atmosphere.

> In most workplaces, NITs will be present, continuously niggling at people's attitudes, often said in jest and in some businesses they become the standard attitude and way of communicating. They do need to be stopped.

Deliberate use of workplace NITs for personal gain

It is also the unfortunate reality that some individuals who undermine others in the workplace use NITs deliberately.

These reasons vary from power to control, to undermine or purely to be vindictive. Pay attention to who is saying what, how that story may change when repeated to other people and the source of the NITs. Once these things are observed the underlying reason may become clearer. It is important that behaviour of that nature needs to be eliminated and everyone needs to understand that it is not acceptable. All staff members should cooperate to recognise the NITs and prevent those statements from going unchallenged.

The typical situations where some staff members may be spreading NITs would be:

- Where a staff member is in direct competition for a promotion
- Where they have a personal issue with that person
- Where they are trying to gain personal power within the workplace by setting other staff members against each other and creating divisions in the group.

NITs may also be created because of a grievance against the individual's superiors. This could be an objection to receiving a pay rise or promotion and the NIT-slinger is trying to undermine that person. The flow on damage to the business and interpersonal relations are very dangerous and this type of behaviour needs to be stopped without delay.

Structured NIT-free culture statements

Using the company's mission and culture statement is a very useful formal document where the standards expected in the company can be stated. This allows the NIT-free expectations of the company to be upheld and spread and acts as a document that can always act as a reference. In the event of behaviours or statements arising that are based on NITs, the culture statement can clearly prove that this behaviour is outside acceptable parameters.

Developing a strong stance in your culture statements also allows all new staff to be educated in the expectations at the time of the interview and brought out again in staff training and staff review processes. Keeping the NIT-free philosophy in the forefront of everyone's minds is required and correcting staff that step out of line otherwise the principles will be forgotten.

Our experience in instituting the NIT-free principles in several businesses has been outstandingly successful. What we found was that certain individuals, who were the most troublesome NIT-slingers in the business who were not willing to change, tended to leave the business naturally. This has happened repeatedly over the years and usually the person chooses to leave of their own freewill, without having to be fired as the requirements of the culture statement are progressively enforced on them. It has been very interesting to see individuals either improving their attitudes and behaviours or they choose to work elsewhere – problem solved either way and no disciplinary actions, letters of warning or unfair dismissal claims!

The culture statements that we have developed focus around several principles including excellence, professionalism, communication, integrity, responsibility, consistency, team work, conflict and systems. Within these statements the NIT-free expectation is clear and issues like gossip, sarcasm, profanity and denigration are specifically mentioned. Being fully responsible for each individual's actions is a cornerstone as well. At the higher levels, expectations relating to happiness, gratitude, balance in life and abundance are also stated so that staff members focus on the higher goals of life and not just on business. A couple of examples are:

- Joy and happiness – I will always make every day a pleasure to enjoy and I will spread that joy and happiness to all those around me, making the workplace fun, positive and a great place to be.

- Balance – I have a balanced approach to life, remembering that my physical, emotional, spiritual and family life is just as important as my financial achievements.

Having a structured mission statement that crystalises the key goal of the company and the culture statements that back up that goal is a useful tool to have on board as it sets the scene and the standards within each business.

Our experience has been that it has also been useful in attracting the right type of staff to join our companies and been a key factor in getting the highest standard of employee to choose to work with us. Having a tailor made range of culture statements that suits each company is really useful and we found that it changed the atmosphere along with NITs training in a remarkably short time.

Staff training about NITs

Education of all staff at every level is therefore important to spread the understanding of NITs. Establishing the culture of having a NIT-free workplace is very powerful, and using the Three Magic Questions will allow staff at every level to recognise the NITs, highlight them and change them into PATs.

We have been involved with the principles of developing a NIT-free workplace in many workplaces and corporate seminars and the results have been extraordinary. The simplicity of understanding what a NIT is and identifying them using the Three Magic Questions alone makes a huge difference in the control of them. That is a great start in a work environment before anything even has to be done actively. Another useful technique is to create a lighthearted sound to go with the NITs, like a foghorn blast, blowing a raspberry, or warning bleeps that create an entertaining episode with smiles all round as the NIT is noticed, removed and replaced with a better alternative.

Dramatic changes to the workplace atmosphere and attitudes have been shown to occur with NITs training in the workplace. Evidence shows that major benefits flow from developing a NITs-free culture in the workplace. These benefits include:

- Staff retention
- Improved productivity
- Increase in client satisfaction
- Improved profitability

It is also interesting that teaching the workers the principles of a NIT-free workplace and culture also leads to a more resilient workforce in terms of dealing with stress, problems and crises. With the rising problems of stress claims and work stress absences, having a workforce that has the skills to manage those situations successfully will also reduce these types of claims and reduce the absences. Research from around the world has confirmed that an optimistic outlook improves the coping ability under duress, and having the NITs-controlling techniques in your emotional toolbox is a great protection for when the going gets tough.

Corporate seminars are available for workplaces of any size, and it is also possible to run "NITs-free days" in the workplace where the NIT-free principles are publicised, promoted and encouraged. Everyone wears "This is a NIT-free Zone" badges or shirts, and with signs in the public areas, the NIT-free education is spread to the customers and therefore into the community more broadly. Anyone that lets a NIT escape puts a coin in the communal "swear box", and the proceeds are given to charity or enjoyed in some positive way like a party, for all the staff. This community education will help reduce NITs in the wider community and also create more loyalty from customers to your organisation. It will help to spread the knowledge of NITs and help to create better work and community attitudes and support the NITs-free message.

Mastering Negative Impulsive Thoughts (NITs)

Dealing with workplace mistakes

Dealing with mistakes and problems in a positive manner is another very important factor in creating a happy and productive workplace. The key factor when dealing with mistakes is to look for the reason the situation arose rather than just attacking the individual who made the "mistake". Studies have shown that mistakes in the corporate and business world occur about 80% of the time due to system errors and only 20% of the time due to human errors.

> So when mistakes or problems arise, look for the reason that mistake has happened and look for the reasons behind the problem rather than just attacking the person who made the mistake.

This will often highlight system errors or may highlight reasons that an individual acted in that way, for example a personal issue or illness that needs to be addressed separately.

Once your workforce understands that four out of five mistakes are system errors and a system error is therefore far more likely, the staff are much more open to report issues and look at ways of improving the systems in the business. When a mistake occurs, focus on what the actual problem is and why it has occurred. What are the systems in place related to the problem – is there a training deficiency, is the person getting the information needed to complete the task, is there a better way to perform the task, is it actually possible to perform the task as expected? If the task is performed adequately by others in the same situation, the individual's performance needs to be assessed. Have they performed better before or have they never been able to do this task?

The key is to focus on achieving a positive outcome and finding a solution to the problem, not just considering that the individual is the problem from the start. By asking the

Negative Impulsive Thoughts In The Workplace

questions in a non-judgemental way, the individuals are not feeling personally attacked and with this supportive approach, a positive solution is much more likely to be found.

Some companies have very severe penalties and complex, extremely unattractive reporting requirements for any incident. This often leads to failure to report, even with quite severe events and almost life-threatening near misses. The big problem with this is that the systems are not improved and exactly the same incident is almost certain to happen again possibly with more damage next time.

Many examples of this have crossed our professional paths over the years. A good example was a mining incident where due to the lack of access to the opposite side of a conveyor belt, a worker climbed across to sort out a problem. He fell on the way across and was almost crushed to death as he got caught in the rollers and was dragged down a chute. The incident was not reported, because the event would result in severe disciplinary action and dismissal as crossing the conveyor belt was against regulations. But the system error was that inadequate crossing points were available to allow rapid repair to the problem on the opposite side of the belt.

Another example of mistakes arising occurs when staff are excessively fatigued or overwhelmed with high-pressure workloads. Over recent decades, fatigue management strategies have been put into place to protect long-distance drivers, shift workers and night workers to allow adequate rest and recuperation between sessions. Yet situations still arise like staff shortages, work delays and home situations that cause sleep loss. These may include young children not sleeping well, illness, divorce and bereavements. In the process of investigating workplace events, these possibilities need to be investigated before making judgments against individuals.

These home situations can potentially be dealt with by using sensible roster planning and having a company ethos that is open enough to allow staff with these situations occurring, to report them and allow ad hoc changes to rostering or hours. Having the inconvenience of roster changes is much more bearable than dealing with catastrophes of staff errors. Without question, that person's productivity and long-term support of your business will be significantly stronger.

> At the other end of the mistake spectrum, is that when a worker does make a mistake, taking full and immediate responsibility for it, is the best policy! When related to customer service, an immediate apology to the client is made by the employee, the error is corrected and flow on effects are stopped.

A typical example is when a receptionist forgets to put a client's file up for an appointment, so the professional is not aware that they are waiting. Time passes and the person in not seen in a timely manner. By immediately taking responsibility and apologising, the receptionist prevents the mistake being blamed on the other staff or the professional. Equally, if it is the professional that is running behind, it should be them that immediately apologises and explains the reason for the delay.

The "ripple effect" is the term used for the effect of damage spreading outwards to affect everyone around when responsibility is not taken. Without an apology, the angry client is unsettled in the waiting room, has a heated discussion at the front desk that upsets the other clients and the other receptionists. They then go in and have an unpleasant consultation and their bad attitude flows them as they go out to pay the bill, spreading the bad feeling to everyone in earshot! All should be stopped at the very beginning with a simple and honest apology at the time of the first mistake!

Potential to prevent suicide

Death rates from suicide in developed countries is around 10-12 per 100,000 people. This means that more people die from suicide than road accidents every year – 20% more in the USA, 90% more in Australia and 400% more in the UK!

Suicide is the biggest killer of men under forty-four and women under thirty-five in Australia, and it is preventable. Suicide rates are also four times higher for men than women. So this is a very common problem and everyone in the workplace can help to play a role and save a person's life!

> Paying attention to statements that are being made by co-workers may identify those that are developing suicidal thoughts. A simple understanding of these features are can allow you to recognise the tell tale signs deteriorating mood and you may be able to help them get help and save their life.

As individuals become more depressed, their thoughts and comments become more negative and derogatory. These thoughts are often aimed at themselves, but they may also be aimed at anyone in work situations or their family. As the depressive thinking becomes more powerful, everything in the persons' lives becomes harder to do and less pleasurable. This often gets to the point where they stop performing hobbies, sports and don't even get pleasure from sex.

Their relationships with their partner or friends start breaking down and this is often used as the reason for them to be feeling down. But the real reason is often the other way around as they are having the relationship trouble because of their depression and negative thoughts. In the workplace, their relationships with co-workers and superiors also break down as they may become aggressive or abusive, or they may become reclusive and withdraw from many social interactions.

It needs to be remembered that the two extremes are the verbally profuse person who has bad things to say about everything, and the person who just shrinks back into their shell and says nothing. Unfortunately, inside the passive exterior of this second picture may be a personal hell that their co-workers don't understand and may not feel able to cope with. However, as their co-worker, enormous help and support can be achieved with the simple sharing of concern for that person. Positive, open and non-judgmental support towards that person may be enough for that depressed person to verbalise their negative thoughts and therefore allow for professional help to be recommended and hopefully obtained.

Unfortunately, there have been many successful suicides where the introversion has never been questioned, and after the catastrophe, everyone feels terrible that "maybe something could have been done". Now is the time to start. Keep your eyes and ears open, recognise those NITs and where they appear to be invasive and overwhelming, encourage that person to seek professional support.

The good news for these people is that although depression is very common, with one in five people experiencing it at some stage in their lives, it can be successfully treated – often successfully improved in a matter of weeks! The difference is like night and day for the sufferer, and the most common feedback that we get as health professionals from people after they have received treatment is that they wish that they had come for help sooner and not suffered the symptoms for so long. It is a very satisfying result to move people from that pit of despair and out into the light, joy and laughter that should be everyone's usual experience of life.

So as the co-worker's "friend" you may:

- Ask questions about how they are going and how are they feeling.
- Mention that you have noticed that they are more

irritable and "cracking up" at the smallest things.
- Mention that their recent behavior is unusual for them and they are difficult to be around.
- Just be open to offer your support or help.
- Quote lines from this book, if necessary, to allow the conversation to be started – or lend them the book!

The worst thing for these people is to be ignored and hope that it will just go away. Never be afraid to ask if they have had thoughts that life is not worth living, of harming themselves or committing suicide. If you can't speak about it, this reinforces the taboo, and when asked if they have had thoughts of death, the person will usually answer the question honestly, even if they underplay the intensity of the thoughts at first.

"A problem shared is a problem halved." Just allowing the person to vent will often help that person. Then some support and advice will make the person feel relieved and purged.

Arm them with a few simple bits of information; you might point out that feelings of depression are very common, but you understand that treatment is very successful quite rapidly and that it can get you out of the black hole. So they should seek professional help and get along and speak to their doctor about it. They should not feel guilty or stupid; it is a simple physical change in the brain that causes these feelings, and it can be corrected with treatment just like high blood pressure needs medication. There are also good quality websites giving detailed information about depression, how it occurs and how it can be successfully treated. Encourage them to see someone for professional treatment – it really works!

> So first pay attention, and then ask questions, offer support as a friend, let them know what you know about how successful the treatment is and if necessary advise on professional help. You may just save someone's life!

Summary

As a full-time worker, you will spend more awake time at work than anywhere else, so let's make workplaces wonderful environments for everyone! The steps to changing the work environment include:

- Educate your staff and co-workers.
- Develop an agreed workplace culture of a NITs-free environment.
- Make it entertaining with the foghorn or raspberry-blowing sounds.
- Run NITs-free days in the workplace.
- Certify your business as a "NITs-free workplace".
- Deal with errors openly and without personal judgment.
- Look for system improvements to reduce errors.
- Recognise and support workers who show any possible depressive symptoms, and help to reduce the suicide rates.

A NIT-free workplace creates rewards for the workers, clients and business owners as business profitability and reputation will outstrip your opponents. Get started now!

11
Negative Impulsive Thoughts In Sport

> "Success is a journey, not a destination.
> Half the fun is getting there."
> **Gita Bellin**

What are the key strategies used by top-level athletes that result in achieving the highest successes in their field? What makes the difference between the winners and the ones that come second? What is the difference between a successful coach and an unsuccessful one? What are the keys to getting team members to act above their average and trust their teammates to fulfill their roles?

Looking at elite athletes, there are many key processes in place across sport and interestingly, success in sport is very much like success in life. It starts with having a passion and a dream that drives the action. From the dream, specific goals and targets are developed with a plan put into place for the training and performance progression. Plus the athlete persists and persists. Behind all of the practical steps in the process is an unconditional self-belief that not only are you able to achieve the goal, but that you will achieve the goal. At no time, despite the setbacks that undoubtedly will occur along the way, does a successful athlete allow NITs in any form to enter their mindset. NITs for a solo performer might include self-doubt, belief that others are better, defeatist thoughts, and self-criticism over mistakes and thoughts that they might never succeed.

Mastering Negative Impulsive Thoughts (NITs)

In the team situation, NITs are much more complex, as a team sport requires cooperative action and 100% trust in the team members to fulfill each of their tasks. So NITs may come with individual denigration like "That person always lets us down," or "I won't pass to him because he often drops the ball." Group self-doubt results in thoughts that the other team is so much better than yours or that you have no chance against them. There is also the possibility of personal conflicts or jealousies that can undermine the team's functioning and may not be evident on the surface.

NITs-free Road to Sporting Success

Elizabeth: *As an example of sporting success, one of our local athletes from Mackay, Ken Ware, won the Mr Universe title in the 1980s. Being a personal trainer, I was closely involved in the process as he was a family member and I was able to observe and assist in his training program. While he would train physically for hours and hours to get his body into shape, he would also train his mind to match the strength of his body. In lengthy conversations about this process, he would go through a focused relaxation process and then visualise exactly what he wanted to happen in the Mr Universe competition. Mentally he visualised right from the start of his routine, including every bit of detail, seeing every step of the process, hearing the crowd cheering him on, and imagining how he would be feeling at the end of the competition when he stepped up on the podium to receive the title!*

This visualisation was completed in detail, with all his senses switched on as he performed repeatedly every day in the lead-up to the competition. He knew exactly how the future was going to happen and he accepted nothing less. In his mind, there were no other options and this was the reality for him without question.

Ken went through many years and many competitions just missing out on the title, due to less than ideal proportions. Despite these setbacks, he persisted and worked on his weaknesses by placing reminders in every room of his house to exercise those areas of his

Negative Impulsive Thoughts In Sport

body that need more proportion. Eventually, his hard work and optimistic attitude (PATs) paid off and he won the Mr Universe title. Persistence, persistence and the never-give-up attitude!

These days this process has now become more commonly used by high-performing athletes and remains one of the mainstays of maximising performance. In reflecting what is involved in this process, it is clear that NITs have no place in the mind of a successful athlete and absolutely need to be eliminated and replaced with the positive alternatives. The smallest doubts and negative thoughts have the potential to sabotage and undermine your success, so they need to be recognised and removed early. Your commitment and belief in yourself needs to be 100%, with the combined belief that you can perform to the level required but also that you deserve the victory.

A nice example of the level of self-belief that can be achieved in team sports was shown when the Australian sailing team made history and won the America's Cup. Back in 1983, despite being the underdog by a long way, the Australian team managed to undermine the confidence of the dominant American team with some mystery and bluff. They did have a newly designed keel that potentially could give them a performance advantage. But they magnified the possibility to the point of having the Americans believe that it was much more than it might be. This resulted in the Americans making a legal challenge to try to have the boat banned. The effect of that was to magnify the Americans' fear and the psychological war had been won by the Australians before the race was even run.

However, underneath it all, the Australian team had prepared with a lot of focused team-building and visualisation of how they would perform as a single, efficient unit with 100% trust and faith in every team member. They visualised how they would perform the maneuvers efficiently and smoothly and cross the line ahead of the Americans. They performed this visualisation repeatedly with strong emotion attached and imagined holding the Cup high above their heads.

The drama unfolded, with the Australian team down three to one after four races. Team USA only had to win one more race from the remaining three, but Australia fought back to three all! In dramatic fashion, the whole series was to rest on this single race, and despite many lead changes in the final race, the NIT-free Australian team crossed the line ahead of the Americans to create history! A public holiday was proclaimed for Australia, and the Americas Cup was taken to Australia for the first time ever! History shows that the American team got its revenge in the next challenge a few years later and the Cup was returned to the USA – but Australia still remembers the victory of 1983!

So let's look at some of the opposite ways of training and operating in sports. Standing at the side of a children's sports game, we have observed the coach of the team yelling at the children when they missed the ball or the tackle. He was telling them that they are "stupid" and "hopeless", embarrassing them and even encouraging them to perform foul play or cheat to get an advantage. Some coaches and parents also encouraged bad sportsmanship and threw temper tantrums themselves, with the idea that they have to win at any cost.

So what are the children learning in these situations?

- They are being personally criticised, so the seeds of long-term self-doubt and NITs are being sown.
- The people who are in the position of being their mentors are teaching them that winning is more important than having a good game, and that cheating, tantrums and offensive language are fine!

While these standards and the personal NITs being implanted are bad enough, even worse is that the underlying reason for playing sport and the underlying benefits are being overlooked, changing the focus from playing the game to winning the competition.

Surely the reason we should be playing sport is to keep fit and active, and enjoy the game? If we are skilled and dedicated enough to get to the highest levels of sport, we should be proud of how far we get. Motivating people with fear and derision is only sustainable for a limited time, until the person decides that they don't like the sport and gives up. Motivation using positive reinforcement, on the other hand, is sustainable, and also gets better results. More importantly, it results in happy children who will go on to be happy adults who are more likely to continue being active, fit and healthy.

Unfortunately, statistics are showing us that around the world less and less people are in the healthy weight range because of lack of exercise and poor diet. This is an ominous sign for the future health of our populations overall, and does bring into focus the importance of keeping active, making sports fun and ensuring that we are all participating. This includes the mums and dads out there as well because you too need to keep fit and active as you grow older. Ongoing exercise will also allow you to keep playing with your children and grandchildren for longer and send the right message to your offspring about the importance of ongoing fitness.

A great example of how NITs-based teaching can push talented children away from their sport is the story of a young dancer who was very talented and won many local competitions as well as having success on the national circuit. Her teachers would constantly point out her mistakes or how certain moves needed to be improved by this action or that movement. The teachers never ever complimented her. They actually never said that she was doing really well or even that she could be very successful! In fact, the lack of positive or honest input meant that she didn't even realise that she was any good, and certainly didn't think that she was talented or anything special! Even though she was winning many of the competitions, all the feedback that she was getting was criticism, pushing to her to do more and completely lacking positive encouragement.

At one point, as a young teenager, she even had great success in a nationally televised talent competition and won the first prize. She also got to rub shoulders with the famous television personalities and high-end performers. On returning to the dance studio, rather than congratulating her for the success and her hard work and persistence in getting to that level, the teacher said in a very demeaning tone, "So if it isn't Miss Talent Time herself! You might have been treated differently down there, but now that you are back here, you are just one of the class and don't think that you are anything special!"

Having started dancing at the age of three and training intensively from the age of eight, doing five hours a day on weekdays and Saturdays till 3pm, her life had been completely controlled by and dedicated to dancing. The children were not allowed to be absent due to injury or illness, and in those situations the child was required to turn up and just watch the class so that they would still "learn" the moves! There was no life outside of dancing, as it took up most of the non-school hours, and the dancers would be exhausted by 8pm – with homework to do after that.

At the age of about twelve, twice-weekly weigh-ins commenced where the teachers would check each girl's weight to ensure that they were not putting on excess weight. These weigh-ins created intense fear from the girls because, if there were any indication of excess weight, the teacher would humiliate that girl in front of the whole class. This was such a big deal for the children that many of them would be putting their fingers down their throats before the weigh-in to try and get their weight down!

Ironically, the girls were at the age where their self-image was at its most sensitive, and weight gain is essential for the development of strong bones and healthy fertility. That is before we even consider issues like anorexia nervosa and bulimia, which actually kill teenage girls today. Flippant comments were often made by the same teacher to students without any understanding of the consequences. These included "You're too fat to ever make it as a ballet dancer," regularly said in the middle of a class in front of everyone. Not only was it embarrassing to everyone in the class, it also led to long-term psychological problems in addition to weight problems for many of the girls. One of the young girls was hospitalised due to anorexia as a direct result and she still struggles with the condition years later.

The attitude drummed into the dancers was that ballet was the most important thing in the world and that they were not allowed to play any other sports. After taking part in basketball for a few weeks and enjoying it immensely, the dance studio found out and forced one of the students never to do it again "because it was using the wrong muscles." So the pleasurable sport ended and the NIT-filled dance studio was all that was allowed.

Soon after returning from the TV finals of the talent show, the dance studio had a visiting teacher attend, and as often happens, extra classes were booked on Sunday as the rest of the week was already taken up. These classes were not meant to be compulsory, but when the dancer was not there at 8am on Sunday morning, the studio phoned her home and demanded that she attend the class even though she had planned a day trip to the Whitsunday Islands. Against her will, she attended, and half-heartedly performed the various moves and exercises. At the point where the dancers were performing the routine where the sequence of leaps and air bound splits occur, the visiting teacher stopped the class and asked this young dancer, "Dear girl, where are all the wonderful grand jetes that I have heard so much about?"

Mastering Negative Impulsive Thoughts (NITs)

The young dancer suddenly had a few light-bulb moments at this point. Firstly, the studio only forced her to be there on her one day off to show her off to the visiting teacher, not for her own benefit. Secondly, if the teachers were saying wonderful things about her to other people, why had they never told her anything like that to her face or ever given her any positive encouragement? It also became clear, several years later, that in grooming her for "greatness", everything the studio had done was meant to be for her good, but they forgot one simple task. They forgot to tell her that she was very good, that they loved how she danced and that their plans were to take her towards great success! Perhaps they were working with the "Treat 'em mean, keep 'em keen" philosophy, but because this is NIT-based, it was destined to backfire.

So after twelve years of dedicated hard work and personal sacrifice, repeated verbal and emotional negativity and in the absence of any significant positive input over these years, this extremely talented dancer had just had enough. The passion had been ground out of her and she walked out of the studio and away from dancing forever. What a shame.

> The moral of this story is obvious, and coaches who are striving for high-performance teams or individuals need to take note: you cannot keep driving people with negativity alone.

They will only take the negativity for so long before eventually taking the easier road of pulling out of that sport and taking up other more enjoyable pastimes. They will realise that doing nothing is more enjoyable than being under intense continuous duress, even if you do that "something" very well.

Third-party NITs used for personal advantage in sport

The use of NITs in sport to create an advantage for your team or yourself is commonly used as a tactic. The recent use of microphones and cameras during play has led to a greater understanding of how entrenched this habit is. In cricket, many teams are passing NITs-based comments to the opposition, especially in order to intimidate or undermine confidence. This tactic is so established that it is called "sledging". This process is widespread across sports, and many psychological processes are used to erode the opposition's confidence or concentration. The comments may be derogatory, demeaning or directly threatening putting seeds of doubt into the opponents' minds about their own skills.

Other common NITs are personal comments about their looks, their weight, their race, their wives, their mothers, etc. These are specifically aimed at annoying and breaking the opponents' concentration, or sometimes to try and get the opponent to react violently so they are penalised.

At a much more subtle level, there are processes performed deliberately by sports personalities just to be annoying and irritating to the opponents. Tennis has great examples of these, where delays or injuries are used to break the concentration if someone is in a losing streak, excessive delays between points, certain actions or idiosyncrasies. The grunting that escalates to a shriek as some of the players hit the ball is completely unnecessary, and has no benefit except to focus the grunter and dominate or put off their opponent.

In the past, we have seen even more outrageous behaviours, like John McEnroe and several others who would curse and scream, throw their rackets and argue vehemently with the umpires. Thankfully today penalties and fines have now limited this. This behaviour can obviously be very disruptive to their opposition unless the opponents had strategies in place to keep their own focus. Most players' performance would deteriorate when they behaved like that too, but in the case of John McEnroe, his performance seemed to improve while often putting his opponents off their game.

Every sports person and team will have to make up their own minds as to whether they want to use third-party NITs to undermine their opponents or if they want to retain their honour and decency and allow the best player or team to win. It needs to be a conscious or deliberate decision, so that everyone in the team knows the culture and expectation and everyone can be consistent within that expectation.

It is also very easy to recognise the "good sport" who in defeat will congratulate their opponent on being better than them on the day, acknowledge their superiority and learn from the experience. The other feature is that if you have given your best shot and lost, you should still be happy with your performance. The "bad sport" on the other hand, will lack grace, blame their injuries, underlying illnesses, the umpire, the bad conditions (that both parties had to contend with!) and any number of other excuses. The difference is that the good sport is actually enjoying the experience while the bad sport is having a bad time, and even when winning probably continues to have negative thoughts and fears that reduce their pleasure in life.

> As a sportsperson, you will need to make your decision as to whether you will use NITs against your opposition, but just remember about karma. What goes around comes around, so it is up to you!

Protection from third-party NITs in sport

Let's now take this from the other side: your opposition in a sport is throwing around NITs in an attempt to get the better of you. How can you protect yourself? The usual processes that you have learned for workplaces and social settings are not likely to work in the sports arena, due to the limited interaction you are likely to have. At most you will probably only have a few words or a single sentence to communicate with your opponent, so the educational approach is not going to work.

There are three steps to help in treating NITs in sport:

- Remember that the source of all NITs is fear.
- Protect yourself from the NITs.
- Make direct retaliation in denouncing the NITs to the opponent if necessary.

The first thing to think about is that anyone using NITs against you is so afraid of your ability in the sport that they need to use NITs to beat you. They do not believe that they can beat you on a level playing field. It's quite an exhilarating thought, really, so keep this underlying principle in your mind whenever you have to deal with NITs in sport. It's the same feeling when the opponent is getting irritated and angry and throwing their racket around. This behaviour reflects their lack of personal control and therefore their concentration will be scattered.

Using the principle that the opponents feel so insecure that they can't beat you without dirty tactics should in itself boost your confidence. But the additional focus required at this point is to keep your focus on your own ability, your own hard work, how well you can play and how you deserve to win. Maintain your integrity and these principles will follow you into every section of your life, including sport. Repeat and focus on your own positive affirmations and block out the NITs that are being thrown at you by your opponent.

If the NITs are in the form of irritations to try and generate a violent outburst, remember the wise saying that, "They can't get your goat if they don't know where it is tied up!" The key here is that even if what they are doing is really annoying you, you need to keep your emotions under control so that the opponent has no idea that they are having any effect. If they get any inkling that their behaviour is getting to you, then they will continue. Yet if they think that their efforts are failing, they will probably stop or try some other approach.

John: *The most dramatic example of this that I have witnessed was during a Thai kickboxing event that I attended as the doctor to deal with injuries. Throughout the fight, the professional Thai boxers would hold a big smile on their faces, no matter how badly they were hurting or injured. As if they were saying to their opponents "That didn't hurt, keep on coming, you can't hurt me, this is fun, what a pathetic punch, take that back, I am OK, how are you?" It was truly incredible to take the pounding that they did and never flinch or show any emotion apart from the seemingly happy smile! So be sure to keep your emotions under control or hidden, otherwise the opponents will know that they have found your "goat".*

The third aspect to consider is whether to retaliate to the NITs from your opponent. Any retaliation needs to be without emotion and based on the "You haven't got my goat" principle: calm, unaffected and with integrity. Some judgment of which approach will have the greatest effect here is useful, because you can come at the response from a number of angles. These include:

- Naming the comment as a NIT.
- Reflecting on how sad it is that they seem to have to resort to denigration to win the game.
- Express surprise at the fact that the comments only need to be made if they are expecting to lose.
- If they are personal denigration-type comments, just reflect it straight back with a comment like "That comment reflects the state of your mind more than anything to do with me! Poor you!" Or you can fall back on the classic "Your opinions are none of my business!"

Other approaches, if you feel the need to say something, are to focus on the game, e.g. "The scoreboard tells the truth!" if you are winning, "Let's see the score at the end of the game!" "Pity you need to resort to comments like that when this is just a game. Let the best team win!" "Wow, you must be really scared that we are going to win if you have to resort to those tactics!"

Summary

Success in sport is dependent on focus, persistence, visualisation and having a NIT-free approach to your sport. Once you have successfully dealt with your personal NITs, you may also have to deal with third-party NITs from your opponents, using the three steps of acknowledging that the NITs come from fear, protecting yourself and then retaliating as appropriate while maintaining your integrity and class act.

Other keys are not letting your opponents see that they are successfully annoying you, so keep your emotions to yourself and have the Thai-boxer approach of always having a smile and not showing any pain that may be underneath.

Team sports require trust and shared vision to take them forward and avoid self-destructive NITs that will undermine team unity and function.

Watch the coaches who teach your children to see if they are instilling quality behaviour and principles, sustainable and enjoyable long-term participation in sports activities. If not, find another coach or another sport!

12
Negative Impulsive Thoughts In Politics

> "If the facts don't fit the theory, change the facts."
> **Albert Einstein**
> (*but the politicians didn't realise he was joking!*)

International politics is one of the most amazing areas for NITs and active use of negativity for personal or political gain. Things seem to have degenerated in the past twenty or thirty years, with many political personalities becoming vigorously adversarial rather than focusing on policy. The basis of the current approach appears to be to attack with antagonism and personal denigration rather than dealing with policy issues.

Very strong personal and group derision seems to have become the norm in politics. The attacks are now so severe that the people on each side of politics seem to be unable to be civil to each other at any time. This then tends to rule out civil relationships across the major party boundaries at the higher levels.

The issues no longer play the central role in political processes. Now the "spin doctors" step in to manipulate the information and create fear and emotional responses to whichever issue is at hand. They will often publicise the smaller issues that create support and suppress the larger issues that are not popular and therefore likely to lose them votes. The result is that the information the community receives is distorted. The politicians seem to be attacking each other with such vigour and malevolence that the majority of information coming from the politicians is negative, personal denigration and full of NITs.

One underlying reason for this is related to the ten-second TV sound bites on the nightly news. A dramatic statement is more likely to be broadcast than an organised and considered argument. The outspoken maverick politicians are loved by the media producers, as it makes their news items much more interesting, and these off-centre and usually NIT-driven politicians will hog the media time. This often results in the retaliation of the same nature to ensure that the opposite side is being broadcast as well.

It's a very sad fact that people are usually more influenced by fear of something bad than a positive emotion of something good. Politicians are masters at generating fear about the policies of their political opponents and the personal qualities of those opponents that are so terrible that a catastrophe will occur. The result is a continuous flow of NITs from our politicians about how terrible it will be if the opposition's policies are implemented or how terrible the opposition are as leaders.

It is also common to see politicians stooping to personal denigration about their opponent's character or past activities, even if these have nothing to do with the current issue or situation. Much less energy is spent in promoting their own good virtues and the wonderful features of the current situation and how the country will thrive and grow in the next term of government under their wonderful leadership.

The result is that both sides are predicting catastrophic economic and social turmoil should the "other side" get in. Of course one side always loses and a significant proportion of the population who believed the rhetoric, then have the feeling of impending doom as they await the predicted catastrophe! This negative expectation in the community has a definite impact on people's confidence as well as business confidence in the economy. The individuals at every level of the community, who make decisions, go into defensive mode and avoid purchasing, investing and growing businesses. In this way business turnover and growth is reduced, which has a direct effect on employment and the state of the economy.

This has a double-whammy effect, because when consumer confidence is eroded, every single individual (as a consumer) loses confidence in the economy or their future employment, as they hold onto their money for a rainy day. This results in an economic downturn completely unrelated to any reality in the economy and is a good example of the power of NITs. Lack of consumer confidence therefore, will cause an economic downturn even in the absence of economic problems, purely by the lack of purchasing and turnover. The erosion of business confidence results in reduced business investment and this magnifies the effect. Therefore, it is very important for our economy, employment and the country as a whole, that NITs are avoided in political debates.

Examples of these types of events are seen in almost every election. The economy slows with the "uncertainty" of the new government and takes some months afterwards to recover. Similar to the fall of currency values when there is an election or when a leader resigns. Since 1888, presidential elections in the USA have resulted in an average of 0.5% falls in the stock market in the two days after an election and this increased to 1.5% with the election of Barack Obama in 2008. The market also fell 1628 points in the 14 days after that election (about 15%) due to negative expectations from political adversaries.

An example of this in Australia was in June 2010 when Kevin Rudd, the then Prime Minister, "resigned" (after he was pushed out). The Australian dollar fell within the week by almost 5% and then rebounded in the next week to the previous level. No other economic factors occurred at these times and the currency and the markets were no weaker or different – it was purely the negative thinking of the "market" (the people buying and selling in the market), which created the panic about what might happen.

The same thing happened when the global financial crisis affected the countries without the banking or economic risk like China and Australia. Again, it was the NITs in the stock exchanges that assumed all countries were similarly affected and that the meltdown would be the same everywhere. This was later proven to be incorrect, and was clearly wrong at the time, as all the financial parameters were good, but people were too attached to their emotional NITs to listen to the hard, unemotional facts.

Politicians are also guilty of generating what might be called policy-based NITs – these are negative or emotionally charged policies targeting the community's fears, prejudices or concerns and amplifying those issues for their political gain. These are usually targeted at ethnic minorities, immigration issues, refugees, successful sub-groups in the community and religious groups.

Good examples of these were the Jews in Nazi Germany, who were very successful economically and socially but targetted by the Nazis out of jealousy. Genocide followed. Successful Chinese traders all over the world have been persecuted in countries that prefer to forget their not-so-wonderful past, from the USA in the Second World War to Australia during the gold rush, South Pacific nations, Africa and non-Chinese Asian countries. Most First Nation races internationally have been racially discriminated against, disadvantaged and had their land taken from them, even though they were the First Nation race. This is often justified by the 'superior' (invading) race creating opportunities for the First Nation but often this was not the case. Thankfully around the world there is now a significant movement to acknowledge the past atrocities and integrate with New Zealand being a good example of honouring the indigenous people. Elsewhere advances are being made with varying degrees of success e.g. in Australia with the Stolen Generation, NT Intervention and other countries efforts to reduce racial discrimination and make amends within the Indigenous communities.

"Ethnic cleansing" has occurred, and continues to be a major cause of war and killing of helpless individuals, without any consideration to their rights. Immigration policies around the world are manipulated and tweaked for political gain often without any regard of fairness for the individual refugee, when a personal political gain can be achieved. The underlying motivation of the politicians in these situations is to gain votes at any cost but they are very unlikely to be open enough to admit it, even to themselves.

Moving to the more sinister personal NITs in politics, the worst type of political behaviour seems to be when politicians attack each other at a personal level and do not focus on the more important issues – these could be called personal-political NITs. Examples are when one politician insults another's appearance, actions, behaviour, sexuality, personal life or personal history unrelated to their political role. This personal NIT-slinging (public denigration) reflects the extremely low level that the denigrator is working from. It seems that they often occur when the NIT-slinger is unable to provide a logical or sensible argument on the issue at hand, or when they are in fact losing the argument.

So why does this behaviour occur, and why has it not been stopped? The politicians find it easier to be derogatory about the other person rather than to explain the complexities of the issues. This may be because they consider it too complex for others to understand, it may be that they don't understand the issue, or it may even be that they are losing the argument.

Barristers in court are legally obliged to deal only with the issue at hand, and are kept on track by the judge. In parliament, no such requirement exists, and as it is much easier to make personal attacks than actually deal with the issue. As a result most politicians accept the status quo and don't try to change the system.

There is also the protection of the parliamentarians called "absolute privilege," which prevents them from being sued under normal defamation laws for anything that is said in parliament. This essentially gives them free rein to say whatever they like without regard to the truth or being responsible for the damage their false statements may cause. This applies to anything that is said within parliament itself. It is like they are carrying a "get out of jail free" card.

> So it appears that across most nations we have politicians who use NITs freely and without regard to anything apart from their next election victory, even if it means a negative effect on the country or other individuals, groups or ethnic minorities.

We also have politicians who seem at liberty to operate beyond the normally accepted limitations of social acceptability, and in many countries are acting beyond the law with impunity as well. This impunity leads to behaviour that is "interesting" and often lacking self-control and decency at any level. Look at parliamentary discussion times across most nations: the behaviour of our leaders can be offensive and rude, looking and sounding more like drunkards at the end of a big night, rather than a professional team of the country's brightest leaders! In some countries, there have even been physical fights in parliament.

Is this the kind of person we all want to be running our country? Is this the sort of role model that we want to promote for future generations to follow? And are we going to continue to hold up these kinds of people for the positions of highest authority in the land? Does your mind not boggle at the idea that we have allowed this to become acceptable behaviour in our countries, and across the world?

The good news is that there is a solution, but first the problems and the NITs that are the underlying basis for most of these issues need to be recognised, counteracted, and a groundswell of understanding needs to be developed within both politics and the community. With that recognition and the desire to see changes, the changes will occur. Just hold onto that feeling of defiance that these standards are unacceptable and you can be the instigator of the change, whether you are a politician or not.

Eliminating political NITs

To create any change, the first step is to take responsibility for the current situation!

The bad news is that you ("we") are all personally responsible. Until you care enough to demand better levels of behaviour and performance from the people that you choose to have as your local politicians and as your leaders of the country, nothing will change. It all starts with you as an individual, before spreading to the friends you speak to, and their friends, and the broader voting community. You need to vote against the politicians that are rude, offensive, derogatory and demeaning. It all comes down to all of "us" collectively voting and applying pressure to ensure that "our" views are followed.

> So to make change occur, verbalise your concerns directly to your local politician, to your friends, and to the media, and make your voice heard. Only when enough voices are being heard and "we" are making enough noise, will the politicians make the changes. So make them listen, correct them at every turn if they are using NITs or inappropriate behaviour, and vote!

There are upstanding politicians that do behave in a decent and appropriate manner, and some also press for parliamentary reforms and standards of behaviour, but they have not yet been successful in instituting widespread change.

The fortunate thing is that as the community pressure grows, the politicians will feel the pressure, and in order to protect their seat, they should try to remove NITs from their repertoire and improve their behaviour faster than their opponent does. This can cause acceleration of the improvement, but the community ("we") need to keep providing input and pulling them into line any time that they lapse into the NIT comments or behaviour.

Of course it would be really nice if we were to start to get the politicians themselves pulling each other up in the media, so that within the political circles the behaviour modification would be a self-correcting process!

In regards to the comparison of the court system, where questions and comments need to stay on track and relevant to the issue, there is no reason why the Parliamentary Whip or Speaker of the House couldn't have the authority to maintain parliamentary standards at the same level and ensure that the issues on hand are discussed without deviation.

Controlling and preventing parliamentarians from using personal denigration with the protection of the "absolute privilege" of parliament, may be achieved by limiting that privilege to certain stated situations only or perhaps only the issue under debate. When the aim is to achieve honest policy debate and avoid personal, minority or group denigration, specific protections could be put in place in the form of parliamentary protocols that protect the individuals and groups.

If the information presented to politicians are of a personal or derogatory nature and is serious and needs investigation, the accusations could be investigated out of the chamber using the statutory bodies in each country and dealt with legally if required. This process would result in the avoidance of unfounded slander or defamation inside the parliament and would move the serious accusations to appropriate legal channels outside of parliament. In addition the protocols for parliamentary behaviour and arguments to be maintained on the subject under discussion, have the potential to dramatically improve outcomes from parliament. Our leaders might then become our "esteemed and honourable" leaders.

> The royal "we" can also have dramatic effects on pressuring the media to forecast appropriate NIT-free coverage. If we vote with our feet by not watching those offending channels, they will change their content. The media is 100% controlled by viewer numbers, and as soon as you create a mass exodus from the offending channels, they will change their behaviour. Power to the people!

For people living in countries without the true democratic process, it is the mobilisation of the masses and the will of the people that creates change. So recognise the NITs that you are being fed and eliminate them as much as you can. Spread the word of hope, truth and love and the changes will occur when the people are motivated enough to change. History has seen it repeatedly, so good luck!

Summary

Every single politician, local or national works for you – not the other way around. "We" the people – put them into their position of power and they work for us. Make them accountable in all their actions and demand they put forward positive messages and behaviours that are appropriate for the leaders of our country. Raise the expectations and the standards to match the community's expectations. If necessary, have the parliamentary regulations changed to keep the arguments based on the issues being discussed and not allow NITs based attacks on individuals and policies.

Spread the word, make the issue important, be clear about the community's expectations and use your vote. That is the beauty of democracy: if enough people care, changes will occur!

May the political NITs be eliminated into history!

13

Negative Impulsive Thoughts In Religion

> "The difference between a flower and weed is a judgment."
> **Wayne Dyer**

There is an old saying that warns against talking about religion and politics if you want to keep your friends. Well, in this book we are covering all areas, because unfortunately NITs are all-pervasive and spread throughout all sectors of life. Religion is no exception.

History overwhelms us with examples of religious wars and ongoing unrest where the leaders use religion as the reason to go off to war, resulting in death and destruction. From the Crusades to Sectarian violence in Northern Ireland, Hindu and Muslim uprisings in India and many others, it certainly seems that religion is the primary reason for a large proportion of wars. However, when we peel back the layers of the arguments leading to the conflicts, we regularly find leaders using NITs that are unfairly aimed at the other religions.

At the same time, the leaders use religious NITS to motivate and lock in their support from the population with a huge effect and turn one religion against the other! The religious principles appear to be used only as an excuse to promote negative thoughts and feelings towards the other side. Plus, it is always the case that both sides believe that their God is the right one and the others are doomed to "hell"!

Recognising and eliminating religious NITs in the future has the potential to reduce religious intolerance, hatred, disrespect, unrest and finally religious wars. At an individual level, it will save lives, improve quality of life and reduce anxiety levels, whilst at a national level, it will reduce the financial strain on the economy to allow those funds to be spent on improving social support. The ultimate result of NIT-eradication within religions would inevitably end up with complete harmony between all religions, freedom from religious antagonism and the ability of each group to freely perform their religious beliefs and travel their inner path without threat.

These lofty goals need coordinated work from the top levels of religious leaders (hopefully you are reading this book!) and from a large groundswell of the population (us) to understand the ways in which groups have been misled in the past, so that we don't make the same mistakes again and to make sure that history is not repeated. So let's look back through history to see the warning signs and how NITs were used in the past. This way, they will be less likely to be used the same way in future.

In retrospect, it's easy to see that past leaders used religion as the scapegoat to justify their wars. The real reasons for the wars were personal or national gain. It certainly seems that the wars were all about power in some form and not really about religion. Inevitably, one country or religion wanted to have more power in the form of land, money or followers, and they were prepared to kill as many people as it took to achieve their goal.

We can see that the leaders on both sides deliberately generated NITs to justify their point of view and motivate their troops to kill or be killed, and sometimes even perform atrocities of genocidal proportions. Terms used on both sides are usually derogatory: "heathens", "infidels", "non-believers", "Catholic pigs", "Protestant dogs" etc. These emotionally charged NITs are used to encourage their supporters to blindly follow to their potential deaths.

In hindsight, we can also see that the reasons were unfounded and the outcomes were not usually achieved. For example, the Christians didn't decimate Islam, Islam didn't decimate the Christians. Neither the Protestants nor the Catholics beat each other in Northern Ireland and the Hindus and Muslims continue to live side by side in the Indian subcontinent. Every continent has seen this struggle in some form, and all the major religions continue to operate around the world, usually at peace with the ones that they were previously at war with.

Even in civil war, both sides claim that God "is on our side," with the American civil war being a good example of that. Religion has always been a convenient reason given on both sides for the carnage. But if you look more deeply, was it valid?

Were the Christians any better than the non-Christians in the Crusades? Were the deaths in the Inquisition in the name of Catholicism justified? Were the killings of the "witches" in the UK, Europe and USA required because they were really a threat to civilisation? Were either the Catholics or Protestants in Ireland any less guilty of breaking the Ten Commandments in their deadly activities in Northern Ireland over all those years? All of these situations were apparently to protect extremely important religious standards or principles being put at risk by the other side. The bottom line is that the fights and wars were all about power, and no religious principles were ever at risk.

As we move forward into more recent history, the situations are surprisingly similar, but as people have emotional attachment, their perception may be biased. The world is currently struggling with the ongoing Israeli/Palestine conflict, which overflows into various other borders. This conflict is magnified into a religious war by the inflammatory demands from both sides about the religious importance of certain parts of land. The Taliban in Afghanistan and Al Qaeda and similar groups scattered around the world produce ongoing conflict and deaths on both sides in the name of religion. NITs fly from

Mastering Negative Impulsive Thoughts (NITs)

both sides, and we see emotive talk, name-calling individuals following their leader's advice to their deaths with both sides unlikely to win.

The solution only seems to come when the broader community have had enough, instruct their leaders to cease the violence and bloodshed and agree to live in harmony with the other side. This is compromise and mutual respect, and it only occurs when the people recognise the NITs and eliminate them (or change the leaders who use them) and have all their energy focused on living well alongside their fellow human beings. This is achievable. A good example being Northern Ireland, where community pressure gradually built over the years until the ongoing violence became intolerable.

Do any religions actually condone or promote the killing of others? Does war ever promote the principles of the religion it is meant to protect? Is the killing of innocent women and children or defenceless men ever justified by religion because they were on the wrong side of the war? Or is religion just being used to justify the attacks or wars to achieve a gain in some way for that group or individual? These are religious NITs that need to be recognised at their source and eliminated. It is the "esteemed" religious leaders who are often responsible for the generation of the NITs. Clearly they are using their NITs to expand their power base, numbers of followers, income or sphere of influence rather than allowing everyone the quiet enjoyment of the religious experience.

In the event of an impending religious war consider, "Is your religion really under threat? Is there some way that the other religion is going to put your beliefs at risk and take on their beliefs?" Even if some other religion does "conquer" your land and practise their religion around you, and your religion is "the right one" and they are wrong, they will go to hell in the afterlife so you do not need to kill them as they will receive their just rewards anyway! Death will be their punishment, and avoiding having their death on your hands will leave you free to enjoy your religion. That seems to be a nice, simple logic!

> There is also a huge disparity between religious wars and the spiritual understanding of the value of life. All major religions have principles of:
> - "Thou shalt not kill"
> - Non-violence of any kind
> - Non-judgment / Allowance
> - Respect for others (of any religion)
> - Purity of thought (No NITs!)
> - Karma / bad acts prevent you going to "heaven"

All major religions respect the rights and equality of all people without expectation of conversion to their religion. Religions also link your acts in this life to your future ascension to heaven, nirvana or the paradise of the afterlife. Therefore religious wars and killings are contrary to the most fundamental principles of religions and spirituality that they are supposedly trying to protect.

There are many similar features across all the religious beliefs in the world, and while some details vary, there certainly exist more similarities than differences. While the focus in the past has been on those differences, focusing on the similarities in the future would be much more beneficial. After all, it seems that everyone is striving for the same outcomes in life, with love, happiness and ascension to the heaven of your belief being the primary goals.

People do not want war, violence, death or aggression, but it seems that we are not yet mature enough as a race to work our way around challenging situations. Just as small children get angry and fight, our history shows a similar reaction at the national level. Perhaps some "growing up" by all nations and leaders with greater patience and negotiation at the highest levels will solve the problems in the future.

Religious texts are interpreted differently by different people, resulting in the same information having different meanings. It is often these differences that produce many of the extreme and anti-social attitudes attributed to one religion or the other. So within each religion, some religious leaders may read the same text and have a different interpretation and put different levels of importance on different aspects of the text. Thus, a very wide divergence of attitudes is found within the same religion and different meanings coming from single phrases. It can therefore be concluded that the problem is not caused by the religion, but by the fallibility of individuals (religious leaders) or the organisations that run the religions (the churches).

A good example of this is the classic religious NITs coming from the apartheid years in South Africa. Some religious groups justified the apartheid laws and suppression of the black majority with the fact that Ham served Jesus in the Bible, and therefore as Ham was "black", the black population should "serve" the white population. The whole society was then based on this premise while the rest of the world danced to a different tune.

Does your religious leader, group or church promote love, equality, allowance, forgiveness and peace for all? Is the principle of "quiet enjoyment of your religious experience" promoted by your leader for your entire group, allowing others to enjoy their different religions equally? Do your leaders lead with the example of non-judgment and allowance of other's beliefs? Do you hear wonderful and positive information from your religious leaders that strengthens your beliefs without fear or negativity and without the need for denigration of other individuals or religions?

> Eliminating NITs from our spiritual and religious lives and from our structured religions themselves is essential for the promotion of harmony and peace in our lives, in our hearts and in our countries.

After all, spirituality is an internal personal and private journey that takes us to wonderful places beyond our current reality. Religion is the formalisation of certain pathways to achieve spirituality, but it should still be personal, private and internal. Achieving your ultimate goal of heaven or nirvana is not determined by anyone apart from yourself, so you can keep focused on improving yourself on your journey. You do not need to change anyone else in any way, especially not by force, violence or killing. This is very unlikely to help you achieve your inner peace and happiness, no matter what any "esteemed" leader says!

The best example of overcoming the odds without resorting to fighting was Mahatma Gandhi with his passive resistance in South Africa and India. He overcame huge challenges from the place of the weakest underdog in society, with integrity, honesty and persistence resulting in the word spreading and seemingly insurmountable obstacles being overcome.

The bottom line is that everyone needs to be aware of, and recognise religious NITs. They have the potential to create devastating effects on their own personal lives, but also potentially damage other people's lives. If everyone is able to recognise, challenge and destroy religious NITs all around the world, all of us and our planet will be better off.

Complete allowance of all religions should be the goal for all of us globally. Any religious leader who puts forward any policy, attitude or statements that lead to inter-religious disharmony, aggression or violence is displaying a non-spiritual path and should be recognised as such. It is the followers of this person who are giving the leader the power. Yet ultimately, it is the people of the world (us) who need to become more aware, more responsible and take action to transform the world into the place we all want and in which we are all safe and happy to live.

Religious allowance is well documented in the Bible with the Good Samaritan story, and stories abound in everyday life showing how cross-cultural and religious allowance can spread the love and joy.

Elizabeth: *On a trip into Lombok's capital of Mataram in one of the Indonesian islands, I was travelling with four other staff members in our car to buy supplies. With the car already full, I noticed two people on the side of the road who looked like fish out of water. As we drove past them, I asked our local manager who was driving our car; did he know who they were and what they were doing? His response was "They are just crazy – don't worry about them", but I had an urge to turn around and help them in some way. I asked him to turn and go back. Reluctantly, after I repeated my request several times, he turned the car around and returned to where they were still standing at the side of the road. They hadn't moved, so I leaned out the window and said "Can we help you?" They ran to the car and as they came closer removed their hats. Their heads were clean shaven, so I assumed they were religious people of some sort.*

Trying to communicate, half in English half in the Indonesian language, I found out that they were Buddhist monks from Thailand. They were on holidays, having attended a conference, and were heading home, but still had a long way to go. Interestingly, monks do have holidays just like everyone else, but they have to fund it themselves and they rely on the goodwill of people along the way. I told them we were going as far as the city and were happy to give them a ride. I got a disgruntled look from the manager, because the car was already full and the air conditioning did not work.

So with seven in the car, two Buddhist monks, two Muslims, one Hindu, one Christian and myself, it was a melting pot! Very broken English was the only form of communication, and the whole trip was filled with non-stop curiosity, questions, excitement and laughter from all sides. Even the initially resistant manager was joining in the banter, and the barriers were broken down by mutual allowance, despite the different religions and lack of a shared language.

We stopped at the shops, and I instructed the manager to buy everyone a drink. Whilst everyone else drank theirs immediately, the monks stored their drinks in their robes for later. When we came to the end of the road, the monks got out and were saying their goodbyes; I quickly slipped them my loose change as we shook hands. They were extremely excited and grateful and bestowed blessings on us as we drove off.

In the car that day, we were all so different externally, but we were able to be happy and joyous together. If only everyone in the world would behave in the same way. If we aim to treat each other with respect and allowance, focusing on our many similarities rather than our few differences, we would realise that we are all on a journey somewhere. We would realise that as we help each other, we are also helping ourselves.

Summary

All of us are responsible for not allowing religious-based NITs to generate power and influence, regardless of who is generating them or how "high" in the religious order they are. Religious NITs can generate hatred, fear, intolerance, disrespect, unrest, violence and wars, and these have no basis in the real religious or spiritual teachings. They will not result in achieving the pathway to spiritual enlightenment or happiness.

It is therefore up to all of us to listen very carefully to the information coming out of our churches, religious organisations and religious leaders to ensure that what is being promoted passes the Three Magic Question test, and is positive and supportive to everyone concerned. We should all be aiming individually for spiritual growth, regardless of what anyone else is doing. Allowance, respect, non-violence and non-judgment are the keys to spiritual growth in every religion, and unless we are personally progressing down this path and ensuring that our leaders are following equally high paths, we should consider changing our leaders!

A world that lives in harmony and peace and free of religious NITs therefore remains the responsibility of every one of us!

14

Negative Impulsive Thoughts In Mental Illness

> "The statistics on sanity are that one out of every four is suffering from some form of mental illness. Think of your three best friends. If they're okay, then it's you."
> **Rita Mae Brown**

It is clear that everyone experiences Negative Impulsive Thoughts throughout their lives, and you will know by now that it's how the person deals with the NITs that determine the effect they will have on your life. However, when a mental illness is present, the frequency, strength and unpleasantness of the NITs increase dramatically and the effects of the NITs on that person's life can interfere with the person's normal functioning.

Most people who suffer with mental illnesses, at the start, think that these feelings or thoughts are "just in their mind". They believe the thoughts are "just their imagination", "just because they are being weak", "something that they should just snap out of" or other naïve beliefs. There are, however, very physical reasons for these thoughts and feelings to occur. Mental illness occurs because of physical changes in the brain that lead to abnormal thinking. All these previous thoughts are therefore completely wrong and inappropriate and fall in to the NITs category.

Mental illnesses result in a variety of symptoms. However if you are suffering from overwhelming NITs that invade every aspect of your life and seem uncontrollable, you do need to consider the possibility of an underlying illness and may need to be assessed by your family doctor or counsellor. Medical professionals are experienced in differentiating poor attitude or "just feeling down" from mental illness. Either way, you win, because if you do not have a mental illness, you will be given strategies to improve your attitude, eliminate NITs and feel better! If you do, you can then receive the specific treatment that will control the illness and make you better.

Suffering from overwhelming NITs – could it be depression?

Depression is the most common form of mental illness and is caused by a measurable and physical change in the brain cells. In fact, it occurs in 20% (one in five) of people at some stage in their lives. This makes it one of the most common illnesses, but it is largely kept private due to old-fashioned stigmas. Depression is a physical illness, just like high blood pressure, although the symptoms in depression are in your mind. The physical change is that the brain's nerve cells become deficient in their chemical messengers or neurotransmitters, with serotonin being the main chemical that is affected. Just like any other illness, depression needs to be effectively treated to correct those physical changes in your brain so that you will get better.

A measurable reduction in serotonin levels is found in depression, and it is really interesting that falls in serotonin also occur with fatigue, lack of sleep, alcohol excess, after surgery and after childbirth. In some people the fall occurs for no apparent reason and is completely beyond anyone's control. There is, therefore, no need to feel guilty, inadequate or stupid for getting depression, but people often feel this way. They are often reluctant to see their symptoms as being real and are consequently resistant to taking medication or receiving counselling, which can lead to a delay in treatment. Treatment is very successful, so early recognition is important to allow a quick recovery and prevent more severe symptoms occurring.

The physical result is that the nerve cells are unable to make the connections with the other cells. This means that messages do not get through and the normal links in the brain don't connect. This very physical change, results in changes to the thoughts, memories, and the interpretation of information. Plus it can also affect the way the physical body functions, as well as the physical processes controlled by the brain. The classic physical changes are the slowing of physical response times, for example, when faced with an emergency in the car, the messages take longer to get through from the brain to the foot to press on the brake – these delays can have disastrous results. Other physical changes are the slowing of other body processes, like the bowels with constipation, reduced energy and physical slowing down of walking, talking, writing and typing. An interesting description is that it is like living in syrup, as everything that you do is hard and difficult, and you struggle to push your way slowly through even the simplest of activities.

The mental changes are more obvious as more connections are lost. The person may have trouble concentrating, poor memory, reduced motivation, sleep changes, low energy, the feeling of impending doom and the lack of desire to get up each day. They will usually also feel that they are personally worthless and feel guilty about many things in their lives – a useful clue for trying to differentiate hormonal teenagers from depressed teenagers. As the symptoms progress, a feeling of life not being worth living can occur, and thoughts of suicide and actual desire to die can result. We need to get people to recognise their own depressive symptoms or the symptoms of their partners, friends or work colleagues so that they can be treated before they harm themselves or others.

The dramatic change that occurs in people with depression is that the NITs that pop up in their thoughts, which they would previously have dismissed as irrelevant, now become the major focus of their lives. It is common to see people bring up events from years before that they had previously dismissed, but which now bother them significantly. It might be how they mistreated a friend, how they were abused in the past, how they were so bad that they lost a job, how inadequate they were in looking after their children or any experience from the past that ended poorly. These events now become proof of how "bad" a person they really are. In this situation, they forget that everyone has learning experiences and they are unable to forgive themselves for past behaviour.

It is also very interesting, in dealing with the depressive person, that they will take the negative pieces of information as being correct (e.g. you are fat/ useless/ ugly/ a bad partner, etc.) and ignore positive inputs (e.g. you are a wonderful parent/ beautiful/ strong/ my ideal partner, etc.) So in this state, the depressed mind is acting like a filter, accepting all the bad information (NITs) and rejecting all the positive information. This is exactly the opposite of the way the brain should be operating, with the filters picking up all the great information that will take you forward and upwards. Instead, the brain is accelerating the downward spiral into the black abyss of depression.

NITs therefore abound in depression and they multiply and become progressively more established in these people. As the depression deepens, the negative attitude expands progressively to affect almost everything in their lives including their work, friends, relationships and their enjoyment of everything including sex. The depressed person will typically be feeling or saying that they are useless, worthless, ugly, and fat, a poor worker, and don't deserve good things in life. They may also be saying things like "why do you bother staying with me?" If these sound familiar to you or you see someone else feeling like this, then consider depression as the cause.

This attitude in life leads to a downwards spiral, and the person can progressively withdraw or not function as they should in their work or life. These symptoms can be vital clues to their friends or work colleagues that depression may be occurring.

This complete imbalance of NITs, without any regard for the positive input, needs to be taken seriously as a person may be at risk of suicide.

So what should be done? If you are identifying with all these feelings and thoughts, go and see your GP or doctor, who can discuss your symptoms. Other illnesses can produce very similar feelings as well, so it is important to be diagnosed by a health professional. Treatment options can be discussed, and more information is available from various websites. However please make sure that you use information from reputable medical sites only.

If it is a friend or work colleague, how should that person be approached? The first thing is that you must not ignore it! Speak to the person, and be honest about what you have observed. They may have:

- become very aggressive or irritable,
- shown a reduced ability to cope with their work.
- become more of a recluse.
- stopped talking to others in the workplace, etc.

Ask them how they feel and offer your support as a friend. Just offering your support may be enough to get the person to start describing what is going on, or it may be the offer that makes them call you before they commit suicide.

Don't underestimate the power of a helping hand or offer of support, even if you think you "know nothing."

If they are unwilling to talk, just leave the door open and say that if they ever need some help to let you know, and keep a friendly eye on them over time. If they are willing to talk and the feelings they describe are similar to the ones described here, share the information and encourage them to see a doctor.

Getting treatment for depression can:

- ○ change the blackness into light.
- ○ get people out of the pit of despair or out of the feeling of struggling through syrup.

It is like turning the light back on in their lives, and the change is often staggering.

In medical practice, we see people coming out of deep depressive states over a month or so, and the most common comment is that they wished they had started the treatment sooner.

The NITs in depression are the result of the illness, and as the depression lifts, the NITs return to "normal" and are controllable with all the techniques available in this book. Overwhelming NITs may therefore be a sign that you have depression. Remove the depression and the NITs will settle down to "normal" levels too.

Illogical NITs, phobias, anxieties and psychoses

Phobias are defined as the unreasonable and excessive fear of everyday events or situations. They are NITs that have grown so strong and established that they leave the person powerless to deal with that situation. Fear of heights, confined spaces, open spaces, other people, needles, spiders, frogs, dogs, snakes or anything in the everyday world can cause this intense reaction. In a person who is otherwise well, without any other mental health issues and no other loss of connection with reality, the phobia may have been triggered by a bad experience in the past.

There is a wise saying that "An incorrect thought associated with strong emotion cannot be removed with logic alone." So it is with phobias, which are sometimes mildly annoying but they can also be so severe that people are trapped in their houses or unable to go to supermarkets, drive a car or fly in a plane.

The embedded NITs need to be treated with one of a variety of processes that replace the associated emotion of that phobia with a different emotion. Some of these processes can be achieved successfully in a single sitting or in a series of sittings. Although some follow-up reinforcement processes will sometimes be required to lock in the new emotional association, the change should be permanent and long-term. The specific therapists that perform this work are hypnotherapists, NLP practitioners and psychologists, so look for a reputable practitioner near you.

Anxiety, stress and panic disorders also have frequent and intense NITs, with strong negative emotion attached that is out of proportion to the situation. Anxiety itself is a self-protective mechanism. Anxiety can be triggered when the person is placed in a risky situation where their safety is threatened and the fight or flight reaction kicks in. This aids the person's run to safety or fight with the "danger," but in these conditions the fear is inappropriate to the real level of risk involved.

The other consequence of excess stress in our society these days is that we are not burning off all the excess adrenaline or sympathetic nervous system activation that the stress reaction produces, as we generally live a sedentary and inactive life. The whole purpose of the reaction is to prime the body and mind to fight or run, and that is what we need to do when we feel stress building up. Vigorous exercise is therefore the antidote to stress, as it will burn off any built-up adrenaline, sugars, or fats and use up the sympathetic nervous system's activation. This returns the body to a more normal and healthy level of functioning.

Obviously there are also practical processes that can be achieved with relaxation, meditation, counselling and psychotherapy to avoid or reduce stress feelings. We recommend that you use these in combination with vigorous exercise for added benefits.

Panic disorders are where people experience strong anxiety and stress reactions frequently, with or without specific triggers. These panic attacks can render the person paralysed with fear. Again, similar to phobias, these will probably need professional help in the form of therapy or medical treatment. This treatment is especially important if the panic is occurring frequently and interfering with everyday activities or enjoyment of life.

Psychoses, on the other hand, are abnormal thought processes where the person is unaware that the experience is not real, and this is caused by the mental illness itself. The nature of these thoughts can vary from minor to severe, and the experiences can be visual (seeing things), auditory (hearing things) and delusional (beliefs that are unreal). Examples of these thoughts include:

- They see or hear people around them that no-one else is aware of.
- The imagined people may talk to them or amongst themselves.
- That they are being controlled from the outside.
- People are trying to get at them.
- They have supernatural powers of some type, e.g. that they are God.

These thoughts that can be confirmed by others to be incorrect are hallucinations or delusions, but the person has difficulty differentiating the real from the unreal. Unlike NITs, these psychotic thoughts require assessment and possible medical treatment from a doctor or psychiatrist.

Recognising, controlling and eliminating NITs is still important in all of these conditions, even if other treatments are required for the underlying problem. NITs may continue to pop up even after the condition is resolved in the same way as they do for the rest of the population.

Summary

In mental illnesses, NITs can become overwhelming, and when this is the case and "normal" processes seem to fail in their management an underlying mental illness needs to be considered. Talk to your friends or work colleagues if you see a change or deterioration in their thoughts. With increasingly powerful NITs invading their thoughts or reactions, for anyone having trouble dealing with negative thoughts, get in early and see your local health professional to discuss how you feel.

When you see someone else behaving unusually and below their usual level, encourage them to see their family doctor or a counsellor who can check them over to see if something more sinister is going on. If anyone is struggling to cope or having symptoms that interfere with their daily functioning, get professional help and be checked out.

15

What Is The Nits-Free Road To Success And Happiness?

> "Patience, persistence and perspiration make an unbeatable combination for success."
> **Napoleon Hill**

Success is interesting. Why is it that some people seem to be the lucky ones and always fall on their feet? Even when they have setbacks, they seem to land on their feet again. They are the type of people who enjoy the riches of life and have achieved success in their chosen field. One success is followed by another, and everything just seems to work. Other people seem to keep on struggling, always seem to fail and have catastrophes following them round.

To the outsider, there is the perception that the "lucky ones" don't really have to try and all the success just happens without effort. Others see the successful people as being able to command very high fees for services, easy access to promotions and the good name of the person then sells the next product. It is also perceived that some people have "overnight success" in the music industry or in writing a bestseller, but the sudden success of the first novel of many authors was often preceded by multiple rejections by publishers. Thus, the success that appears to the public to be overnight is usually preceded by many years or decades of hard work, persistence and mastering the skill.

So what is the difference between the successful people and the others? What are the keys that open the doors to success

Mastering Negative Impulsive Thoughts (NITs)

while others seem to follow pathways with less success? Many studies reveal that it is not because of your place of birth, your family, your education, your skin colour, your family wealth or your religion. This is clear from looking at the different successful people that have come from every group and situation; it is controlled by something much less predetermined. This is great news for most of us, as it means that wherever you start in life does not determine where you will end up! And where you end up is completely within your own control and determined by your own beliefs and actions in life.

So what is it that makes the 5% successful and achieve so much more than the other 95%? There are many books dealing with this subject, and the answers are generally the same: it all comes down to you developing a "success attitude", and this comes with several key features, some of which we have covered already in this book. This "success attitude" includes taking full responsibility for where you are now and where you are going in the future. It means that you move from being a victim of your environment to being the cause of things that happen and the driver of events in your wonderfully exciting future.

Successful people will always:

- have very clear dreams.
- have specifically developed goals to work towards, so that they can focus on their actions and do the things that will make a difference and keep them on track to their desired success.
- have a passion for what they are doing.
- channel all that positive energy into creating the wonderful future that they have in very sharp focus in their minds.

This passion drives their actions, they take action and persist with 100% commitment and then continue to take further action even after repeated failures.

The reason that the successful people are perceived as being the "lucky ones" is that they are only seen after they have achieved success and are "suddenly" famous – the fifteen years of hard work before the breakthrough is not seen. The multiple failures and struggles are not seen either, as most people who have achieved success have failed many times in that process. Sometimes the magnitude of this failure would overwhelm the other 95% of people who would just give up and not look for ways to overcome that stumbling block. To the successful person, the failure is a learning experience to improve and modify what they do and teach them what does not work.

Obviously, looking back through all of these features, the key is that the successful people have eliminated NITs from their thoughts and focus on what they can do, rather than what they can't do. They focus on how great it will be when they achieve their success and not on what hurdles are in the way. They focus on why they will succeed, and not on why they cannot succeed! This is all about developing a NIT-free approach to life and their dreams, and taking the simple but persistent action steps to move towards their goals.

Stumbling blocks to success

This late in the book, it is a struggle for us to actually even write more NITs-type thoughts, but we will give some examples of how some people think and how NITs are the fundamental things that cause failure rather than success. You will see that sometimes things "happen" to cause the failure, but there are almost always NITs behind the actions or lack of action that leads to that failure or lack of persistence. So let's look at some of these failure-generating NITs.

Mastering Negative Impulsive Thoughts (NITs)

The underlying belief that you do not deserve success or cannot achieve success is the most common NIT. "I will never succeed", "I am not good enough", "Others are so much better than me" and other self-defeating NITs will undermine your success and cause failure along the way. When failure occurs it proves that perception is correct if that is what you believe. Your self-love, self worth and self-belief need to be strong and secure. Use mentors to match and mirror if you don't yet have enough belief in yourself.

Plus using affirmations will reinforce your good qualities, determination and belief that you deserve success. Take action and learn from mistakes, and then take more action with those new learned skills and this will reinforce your belief that you are on track and that you are following what the successful people have done. So keep doing it and success will follow!

Obviously, you have to develop your specific dreams of where you want to get to with strong emotion and intense passion attached. Keep that dream out in front of you to motivate you to keep taking the action steps. It is interesting how many half-built boats there are in the world, where people have started with the dream of building their own boat, and then ran out of energy or drive part way through. That feeling of having such a huge task ahead is well known to us, as we have dealt with many time-consuming jobs, including building a 42-foot sailing catamaran from scratch.

John: Building the catamaran took three and a half years of continuous work almost every evening, weekend and most holidays. I would finish a full day's work, grab something to eat and after the children were in bed, would go to the shed and work from 8 or 9pm to midnight or 1am - as well as full days at the weekend!

The dream that I had in my mind was having the completed yacht moored on a tropical island, crystal clear water beneath, coconut palms swaying gently on the beach and white fluffy clouds drifting gently overhead as coral trout cooked on the BBQ out the back and we relaxed in the shade and peace. This vivid image kept me going when I was covered in dust and sweat, with glass fibre prickling my whole body. When people say to me "Oh, you are so lucky to have the boat", you may see one side of my face rise slightly in a wry smile as I think, "Luck had nothing to do with it. It was all persistence, hard work and keeping the dream alive!"

Another example of focusing on the solutions to the hurdles that are presented and not allowing the hurdles to be thought of as impossible, was when we were building the Mackay GP Super Clinic. This 1350-metre-squared multi-disciplinary health centre was to house the full range of medical, dental and allied health services in our town. We had an unconditional contract on the land that was due to close within a month. The global financial crisis had just hit, resulting in the banks changing their borrowing policies from allowing 5% equity to requiring 30% equity. Suddenly my friend and financial partner withdrew because someone had just offered to buy him out at a great price. So then I was faced with the prospect of having to pay out 30% of around $7 million for the whole project rather than the original plan of 5% of half the amount – rather a different position to be in!

The land deal had to be closed within a month, and the 30% of this amount was needed immediately. Our focus and main question that we were asking at this time was "How can we do this? What is the solution? How can we pay out the cash of close to $1/2 million (the 30% of the land price) and then find the other $1.65 million cash over the next 12 to 18 months?"

We did not let NITs kick in and think the self-defeating thoughts of "This is impossible. There is no way we can get this sort of money in this short amount of time! In the middle of the GFC, no one will be able to support the project! There is no way to get this done..." Thoughts of that nature would have resulted in failure of the project and loss of our deposit on the land. As well as potentially being sued for the land price anyway, as the contract was unconditional. NITs were not allowed in, and our focus and energy was deliberately and specifically targetted at finding a solution, remembering the saying, "in every catastrophe, there is opportunity!"

Clearly we needed a partner to come on board to replace the partner who had pulled out, as that had to be sorted within a month to get the money on the table. I put together financial budgets and cash flows with explanations of the project and then targetted specific individuals amongst the people that we were directed to, and rapidly found a replacement partner. Hallelujah – we completed it in time to avoid defaulting on the land, losing our deposit and getting sued.

The next hurdle was the requirement of 30% equity now for the whole building. The time frame to sort this out was over the build period, which became about eighteen months due to delays with council approvals and a very wet rainy season that year. During this time, we secured all the tenants for the building with legal contracts in place and I was working very long hours and desperately trying to save money to get enough to avoid having the whole project go under, due to lack of funds. Keeping focussed on the dream, we worked hard to generate the money, but expenses in building that were not expected kept hitting us over and over again.

Persistence, persistence, persistence! The solution, when it did arrive, came from an unexpected direction, and this is often the case when you are driven with passion for an outcome. It turned out that the bank did not require 30% of the actual cost of the land and building but 30% of the value of the building after completion. With the tenants' leases in place, the valuation was based on the income from the leases, which was higher than the actual cost of the building, so we were saved!

Amazing! Set your mind to it, approach it with passion and persistence and opportunities and solutions present themselves that you would never have imagined!

What Is The Nits-Free Road To Success And Happiness?

North Sea Storm

John: *Persistence is also needed in some challenges in life that you may get yourself into but then just have to get through them as there is no other way out. With our passion for sailing, it is always going to be a possibility that a storm will come up that you have to deal with and while you can do all the right things and look at weather charts and forecasts, life just is not 100% predictable. One situation arose when sailing from Scotland to France in the North Sea in early summer when the weather shouldn't be too bad. On this occasion a storm was forecast for the next day so we decided to head off and get one day of travel in and get into a harbour to sit out the storm.*

We left before dawn to catch the tides and favorable winds from the north but within 4 hours, the forecasts had changed and the storm was now going to hit within the next 4 hours! There was no way of sailing back against the growing storm to get back in to the harbour we just left so we had to sail south, with the wind and storm to the next safe harbour about 8 hours sail away. No choice really, we just had to literally batten down the hatches and get through it....

The wind steadily increased in intensity and the cold, dark North Sea waves started building up in size and the frequent white horses progressively changed into breaking crests and surfing type waves. It was the most amazing (scary) experience of my life with us being in a 27 foot yacht, a Mirage 27 with a mast that was probably about 30 feet high and the tops of the waves were at least 3 times higher than the mast! I would look up at the tops of the waves towering above the boat and look back to see the breaking crests of the waves rushing towards us and just hold on and steer the boat straight down the waves so we didn't get twisted sideways and be hit by the waves side on which would undoubtedly result in the boat being rolled over.

Very quickly I realised that looking back at the waves was not really helping and that I needed to just focus on keeping the bow straight down the waves and keeping the stern to the breaking crests. I did not need to look to know when the next wave was coming because the noise of the roaring crest was deafening and looking forwards, you *could see the deep trough of the wave in front of the boat stretching at least five boat lengths downwards! Next the roaring builds up to a crescendo, white froth starts to vigorously wrap around the boat, pulling it violently to the left and right and the violence eases as the crest passes by and go sliding down the rear side of the huge wave. If you don't get it right, the wave catches the boat from the side and the boat will roll a 360* capsize as the keel trips you up. Good motivation to keep focused and steer well, holding the boat face directly down the waves....*

The spray from the seawater was being driven horizontal and stung my eyes and face to the point that I could not look into the wind. The wind was blowing streaks of foams along the black coloured, sinister looking waves that were now mountainously high with the crest breaking and cascading down the front face like a beautiful avalanche – only beautiful after the event mind you!

As the crests grew larger, they started to break into the cockpit and over the top of the boat, sending us reeling forwards and down onto the floor of the cockpit as the boat catapulted forwards at even greater speeds. Holding our breath until the water cleared, we still had to keep the boat on course while it felt more like a submarine than a yacht. The boat would then shake itself clear of the water as we popped back up to the surface and waited to face the next one! This was happening over and over again, with different degrees of severity but with repetition, we got better at coping with the process.

The amazing thing was that the boat itself was doing fine – extra lines and a drogue were put over the stern to limit our speed and the hatches were keeping the water out of the hull. My realisation through this experience was that the boat was going to be fine (as long as it was handled correctly) and that it was people that needed to be strong and not crumble emotionally! Again it is all about focusing on the job at hand, not letting NITs invade your emotions and obviously pay attention and learn from everything that is happening.

Just before dark, we could see the harbour entrance open up and finally we got out of the horrendously large seas into flat water. After such a physically and emotionally exhausting day, it was SO NICE to be in flat water! We moored up, had a hot shower, a hot meal and perhaps even an alcoholic beverage and went straight to bed for a well earned sleep!

So after you have been through a relatively awful experience like that, most other storms seem "not too bad", your confidence in your boat and your own abilities will be greater too. We will certainly work hard to avoid ever being in a storm but if it does happen, we will be more prepared and more skilled. All your major catastrophes in life can be used as learning and strengthening experiences – "What doesn't kill you, makes you stronger!"

Life gives you the lessons you need to learn!

There is a spiritual belief that if there are lessons for you to learn, you will be faced with situations that allow you to learn those lessons. If you fail to learn it first time, you will be given more and more situations of the same type but of a progressively more severe nature. Therefore, if you are being faced with the same sort of problem repeatedly, think about the lesson that you need to learn within that situation. When you learn the lesson, those situations will resolve.

Elizabeth: *An example of this was a good friend who never valued himself enough to stand up for himself at work or to put himself forward for promotions. As a result, he was always being given the jobs that others couldn't handle, or he would be required to help others complete their tasks. At the same time, everyone else was getting the promotions and he was repeatedly overlooked. Only when he started to recognise the pattern of what was happening, did he reflect on the past events and see the underlying problem. With our help, he started to value himself and others started to respect his time. This was achieved by learning the art of saying "no" with key phrases like "Sorry, but I am not able to do that at this time" and "Normally I would love to help you but at this time, I am unable to." As a result, he was able to get home on time, and amazingly, despite working* *shorter hours, got the promotions that he always deserved! It all starts with you valuing yourself.*

How this process works does not matter, but take notice of the underlying problem if you are faced with the same situations over and over again or repeating patterns. Forget the faces of the people involved, as they are just tools, but there is a lesson in there that you need to learn. You just have to work out what the lesson is for you.

NITs and happiness

While success is tangible to each individual and often measurable, happiness is neither tangible nor measurable. It is a feeling or attitude rather than a result. As the old saying goes, "Happiness is the journey, not the destination."

Our experience is that the whole atmosphere and attitude of individuals, groups and workplaces can be instantly transformed from being negative to being positive, happy and supportive. This can be achieved by understanding the difference between NITs and PATs, limiting negative comments and thoughts about others and focusing on the solution and stop the blame game. Also having a plan in place to solve a problem makes you happier because you know where you are going.

> So happiness is not about having every single problem solved and a life absent of any challenges, but rather a state of mind. This is where you see things around you positively and have active solutions to the things in your life that you want to change.

What Is The Nits-Free Road To Success And Happiness?

The problems aren't sorted yet, but you or the group is happy because the decision has been made, the plan is in place and you know that successful resolution of that "problem" is on track.

> So eliminating NITs from your thoughts and your life is one of the most important steps in achieving happiness, and the steps explained through this are a very simple way of recognising them: the Three Magic Questions and the Stop, Drop and Roll technique.

Many books have been written about thinking positively, but the struggle people often seem to have is that they don't recognise the negative thoughts when they have them and previously didn't have the tools to eliminate them. Well, now you do, and as long as you use the tools in every aspect of your life so that they are automatic and maintain your NIT-free attitude, your path to happiness is assured!

As we have said before: "The only limitations in life are the ones you place on yourself."

Summary

Success and happiness are available to everyone. The established pathways and principles need to be followed and the action steps need to be taken with persistence, passion and belief. A "success attitude" needs to be developed, where you have the self worth, self belief and self-love that you deserve it. Your dreams need to be highly emotionally charged and you need passion to drive your actions. Specific goals need to be developed so there is a clear action path to progress along and the action steps need to be taken persistently and continuously to allow the progress to be made.

The main stumbling blocks to success and happiness are NITs that need to be recognised and eliminated from your mind. If you are repeatedly faced with similar challenges in life, look for the underlying pattern and find the lesson in life that you need to learn.

Happiness is a state of mind and can be achieved before the dreams are realised, so enjoy every step of the journey to your ultimate huge success!

16

Where Are They Now?

> So what happened to all those people and those situations throughout the book?

So what happened to all those people and those situations throughout the book?

Well, the "boy" (buoy) in Gili Trawangan still gets dragged under the water whenever the tide is running strongly, and the extra length of rope makes it easier to tie our boat up to it! No harm done, thankfully, and we affectionately called him "Bob!"

Jonas, the old man on Hui Island with the obstructed bladder, passed away peacefully and did have a more pain-free passing than would otherwise have been the case; his family was much less distressed as well. When you help one person, the ripple effect goes a lot further than you ever know…

It has happened that both of us have been told by separate people at different times, "You saved my life and thank you so much!" At the time a situation arises, you give advice, help as much as you can and are thankful when the situation improves, but often you don't know the enormity of the assistance you have been. So always do what you can – sometimes the help will be slight and sometimes it will be greater than you can imagine. Never give up.

The leprosy patients in Nepal are still only treating themselves to limit the damage from their illness and not so that they are cured. This is only likely to change when there is a better social security system or the next generation are more educated and can find work to create their own independence. Elimination of world poverty is considered possible by some of the world's thought leaders including Bill Gates!

After the successful delivery of Mia's baby boy in Sakau, we were later informed that there is now a little "Dr John" running around the village! Both Mia and baby John were doing well.

The children in the more isolated areas of Vanuatu are still growing up without fighting and discrimination. The risk to their NITs-free existence is the spread of our so called "civilised" values through TV, internet and other popular media as the world's technology spreads. The deep impression made on our youngest two boys, lives on and we hope that they lead by example, spreading the NIT-free way principles in the paths that they cross.

Clive, who had the wonderful marriage with the woman of his dreams but didn't think he deserved her, went through a divorce and unfortunately, his poor self-esteem seemed to continue to dog his future relationships. Many years have now passed, and it certainly seems that nothing will change in his life until he chooses the moment to change! Letting go of the bad attitudes that have been passed down from his father and eliminating NITs within his own life will be necessary before he can be truly happy with himself. Only after that, can he really make a partner truly happy. We wish him well (and everyone out there like him).

Daisy, the worker who didn't believe you have any control over your emotions, was correct for herself because she chose that path and continued to have no control over her emotions! Her attitude resulted in her moving on to work elsewhere, and it is amazing how a single NITs-slinger in a work environment can change the whole atmosphere and drag others down. On her departure, the workplace atmosphere immediately improved, staff members were happier and client numbers dramatically improved as well! This is evidence of the powerful effect negative influences can have on business turnover. We wish her well and hope that she is able to enjoy life and overcome the NITs that are overbearing for her.

The doctor with the "illegal" accusations at the front reception desk left our practice with our blessing and relief and worked in another practice for a short while before other problems of similar natures arose. A few months later he left the country as it was too much for the next practice as well. Being a NITs creator and drama king by nature, catastrophes followed him around. Until he learns to deal with his personal NITs and not turn simple things into dramas and focus on solving the problems in front of him, he will create havoc and mayhem wherever he goes.

The No-NITs training in the practice has dramatically improved the staff atmosphere and the doctors' attitudes overall, to the point where clients walk in to the practice and comment on the great feeling! The same processes are successfully taught to businesses, workplaces and corporations to great effect!

Jane, the girl that presented to the doctor in the middle of the night with confusion, was found to have viral encephalitis and after several days being near death in ICU on ventilation, thankfully recovered.

Karma has an interesting way of showing itself. The relative that falsely accused Elizabeth of having an affair in chapter three was later subjected to exactly that experience herself – her husband had an affair! She subsequently got divorced, with her thoughts and words creating her own future and this certainly became the worst experience of her life. She is forgiven by Elizabeth and everything was left to karma, which ran its circle with those interesting consequences!

Tall Poppy Syndrome will continue to be an issue for all successful people, but once you can see the underlying fear and jealousy that is creating it, it is much easier to let slide by! The greater the success, the greater the chopping at the ankles, so just aim to be so tall that all of that is so far beneath you. They can't reach you, so let your integrity and class shine through.

Charleen continues to not take responsibility for her role in the marriage separation, and continues to blame everyone else, alienating many of her friends and family in the process. With this ongoing NIT-based attitude, she has also been unable to attract a steady and meaningful relationship, but with time, it is hoped that she will reflect and modify her behaviour and thoughts to become the wonderful person that is hiding inside the vitriolic and negative shell that pushes everyone away.

Matt has continued to live a healthy and positive life with no regaining of weight, and he successfully completed university and blossomed in his personal life. Everyday challenges still occur, but he now has inner strength and knows that when he wants to get something done, he can succeed. He is now happily married and running a successful business and his life continues to open up for him for a wonderful future with a variety of exciting life plans.

The talented young dancer, who got burnt out after being trained with NITs in the absence of positive encouragement, used her skills of dedication and persistence to good effect in the rest of her life, and took those lessons to help others and spread the word about having a positive approach to life. While having interesting challenges in her own life, she remains an inspiration to everyone around her, by maintaining the most amazing positive approach in all situations! It was, of course, Elizabeth!

17

How Can You Spread Negative Impulsive Thoughts Awareness?

> "Think twice before you speak, because your words and influence will plant the seed of either success or failure in the mind of another."
> **Napoleon Hill**

Imagine living your life free of NITs within yourself, in your family, in the workplace where everyone is positive and supportive, and living in a community and country that reflect the same values and behaviours at every level. Imagine international and religious issues being dealt with using the same positive and supportive processes, and having our media and institutions spreading those principles of harmony, positivity and support for each other.

Is that the world that we all want to move towards? Is that the kind of place we want our grandchildren and their children to be enjoying? If so, then we are responsible for the shift in attitudes and behaviours to move in that direction and keep pushing until that better world is manifested!

If we are going to have an impact on moving attitudes in a "better" direction, we all individually have to be prepared to make a stand for a NIT-free culture, and have expectations that our family, workmates, bosses and higher authorities follow the same standards. So don't let NITs pass you by or gather strength, and make sure that you get them recognised and controlled in some way. Otherwise they will spread, become established and be the accepted truth and status quo. We need to start changing everyone's expectations of what is acceptable and start spreading the education about NITs so that everyone is aware and can prevent them themselves.

Always remember that it all starts with you – all of "us!" Keep practising the skills so that you get better and better at the process, and you can share that skill with others when the need arises. If necessary, attend the No-NITs seminars or retreats where you can hone your skills and sharpen your mind in the processes required. While spreading the word to others is important, making sure that your NITs are 100% under control is the first step! Keep practising the skills while you are out spreading the awareness, as it is an ongoing process – never give up!

Start with your family

Your children will tend to mimic everything that you do and say, and they are probably the ones that you have the most influence over. Make sure that your thoughts, words and actions follow the NIT-free principles. When they verbalise NITs in their words or actions, perform the Stop, Drop and Roll process to show them how it's done. They will then take that on board as their way of life and do it automatically, with a wonderfully positive and happy outlook on life. It's like the child who, seeing a stranger walking up to the house, says, "Here comes a friend we haven't met yet!"

Spouses are not always as malleable as your children, so slightly different strategies will be needed here. Leading by example is a great start, so ensure that you have your own NITs under control and verbalise the No-NITs approach whenever you can, flipping any NITs into positive alternatives – but do it with love! Have a discussion about NITs with your partner at some appropriate time to make them aware of the principles, so they know where you are coming from. Give them this book to read if necessary. Given that there is no possible downside to the No-NITs principles, any resistance is likely to be NIT-based anyway, so there is very little logical argument against the principles!

Remember to involve your extended family including your siblings, the other generations and more distant relatives. The more contact they have with you and your family, the more important it is to have the NITs addressed, as family gatherings have the potential to be NIT tsunamis if your family operate in that manner. Spread the word, neutralise and flip the NITs into PATs as they occur, and move to a NITs-free approach. Persistent NITs-slingers that constantly overwhelm you with negativity might need to be avoided, but this is a decision that needs to be made with consideration of the family circumstances.

Expanding your sphere of influence

As you start to consider expanding the No-NITs message, the next major area to consider is your workplace. Here you can influence your co-workers and your subordinates, but influencing your seniors and bosses will be dependent on your communication skills and their willingness to change. At the end of the day, the business is there to make profit, and the improved productivity, staff retention and client satisfaction are all good selling points that even the most closed-minded business owner would take notice of!

Aim to move the whole workplace to a NIT-free culture, with those principles embedded in the workplace culture statements. It can be driven from the workers upwards, or can be done from the business owners downwards. When more people start pointing out the NITs that are around and making individuals responsible to retract or flip them, the good attitude spreads. As a result the NIT-slingers keep their thoughts and criticisms to themselves.

"No NITs Days" can be run as events in workplaces where the day of awareness is promoted and advertised and everyone follows the principles, wears badges and places signs up for the customers to be aware of the promotion. Any staff caught slipping out NITs puts money into a "NITs box" and that money is used for a party or to add to the social fund for a later event. The benefit of this is that the business is promoting itself as a positive workplace to the workers and customers and the No-NITs message is being reinforced to the workers. Plus the understanding is being spread to the customers and wider community, and the whole process should be fun and positive.

These "No NITs Days" could be expanded to involve other organisations or wider communities or even the whole country!

Use the same principles in community groups, sports organisations, schools and universities, and spread the positive message with NIT-busting when they occur. Starting to affect the wider groups is where persistence and showing by example becomes the way to influence others.

It's important to approach all situations with a smile, kindness and love even in organisational or institutional settings. When we were discussing addressing negative energy with a Hindu priest in Bali, his advice was that if you keep love in your heart, it melts away the weapons of negativity. Even if the people are trying to do you harm with their negative energy, the love will keep you safe! This philosophy in life is certainly very strong, and we have witnessed many potentially violent situations dissolve into peace by the application of an open heart and a smiling face, backed up by the sincere wish to solve the problem to everyone's satisfaction.

So always keep a smile on your face, love in your heart, don't take yourself too seriously, and have fun!

Vote with your feet (only follow leaders who are NIT-free)

Areas of life where organisations or people rely on our support can be influenced by the majority view. Here we are talking about political parties, city councils, school and university representative councils, media outlets and large corporations. The wider community has more influence or power than is generally realised, because if "we" all have an expectation of certain standards that are not being followed, then our power comes from voting with our feet and not using their services, TV channels, products or political parties. It's amazing how the choice to expect eco-friendly products, fair wages for workers and other socially responsible actions have had significant influence on some companies!

Expanding this principle means that we can influence political parties to have the expectation that their behaviour and performance is socially acceptable and professional. They are the leaders of the country, after all, and they need to act that way, not like a rabble of drunkards. Make them accountable by ensuring that they avoid using personal denigration of NITs to attack their political opponents and avoid using NITs to downgrade the economy of the country that affects us all. Make all sides of politics raise their standards or vote for the alternative "clean and NITs-free" parties.

The politicians need to be accountable at every level of politics, from the national assemblies to the local councils. Publicise the great action of the NITs-free politicians and show up the negative ones publically until they are ashamed enough to modify their behaviour. It's up to all of us to be saying to every one of them at every opportunity that we expect them to behave with integrity, class and in a NITs-free manner, and that your vote will depend on it.

Voting with your feet with the media means changing from television channels that don't have positive, balanced messages and use NITs for drama and increasing interest from the consumer – you! That means you have to start reading between the lines of what is being discussed to recognise that many of the stories use half-truths and extrapolation to paint an awful picture of what might happen and put the fear of God into everyone.

Use the Three Magic Questions to recognise which are the NITs, with the understanding that their job is to make things sound more dramatic, so everything you hear on the television or read in the paper or internet is not necessarily true. Change channels, don't accept having your life filled with unnecessary negative input, and let the organisation know that you feel that way. Then they can start to see the rising wave of rejection of the existing status quo.

Obviously, in the corporate arena, just choosing to buy your products from organisations that follow the better principles is where your power is. Let that company know why you are boycotting their products. The strongest imperative for a company to change is declining consumer support and a falling bottom line! The royal "we" have the power – "we" just need to exercise it.

Where to from here?

Now you are armed with the facts and understand about NITs, how to recognise and treat them. You know the enormity of the benefits of eliminating them from personal benefits of an extra nine years of life, less heart attacks, strokes, cancers and infections. Your happiness and personal relationships will be improved to levels you may only dream of! Your children's lives will be dramatically happier and more productive. Businesses, communities and countries will achieve higher levels of success.

But what are you going to do with this information? How are you going to move forward from this point on? What are your desires in terms of the sort of life that you want to live and experience? How do you want your personal relationship to proceed? What kind of atmosphere at work will you be developing? What changes do you want to see in our country and institutions?

What steps can you take today and this month to make a difference?

What kind of world do you want to create for yourself or for your children? What is it that you want most in life? If you had one wish for humankind, what would it be? Happiness, acceptance and world peace?

> The bottom line is that if we all start now and every one of us follows these principles, they are all achievable! Anyone resisting these principles is being driven by either fear or ulterior motives – this will become clearer as the momentum for better world gains traction.
>
> Deep down, it is peace and happiness that everyone wants, and it all starts with you! You are the key – the "man in the mirror." It all starts with you and spreads with the incomprehensible ripple effect outwards around the world and beyond! So what happens next?
>
> We all live happily ever after!

Warning

This book is not to be left on the bookshelf. Keep reading it and sharpening your skills. Give a copy of this book to someone who will benefit and tell everyone else about it!

Spread the Word for a NIT-Free World.

Corporate Programs and Personal Coaching

Keynote speeches, seminars and workshops are available covering the following subjects:

Personal:

Success	"Golden Steps to Success"
Mastering NITs	The keys to controlling Negative Impulsive Thoughts
Happiness Workshop	Control your mind, your happiness and your future
Stress Management	Stress – it's written all over your face!" and others
Happy Heart	Physical and emotional strategies for a "Happy Heart"
Relationships	"Achieving the Ultimate Relationship"

Corporate Development:

Work / Life Contentment	Achieving happiness with high performance
Creating Happy Workplaces!	Achieving positive workplace attitude
Conflict Resolution	Positive solutions to workplace problems

Profit Through Positivity	Improving productivity through cultural change
Workplace Resilience	Using positive attitudes for a resilient workforce
"No NITs Day" at work	Set up and run these events
NIT Free Leadership	Giving your leaders this revolutionary edge
Are You OK, Mate?	Suicide protection in the workplace
No More Dramas	Problem solving without drama or emotion

Retreats

Health and well-being retreats are run regularly – see website for up to date schedules

"Mastering NITs" (Negative Impulsive Thoughts) – achieve internal happiness with self-empowerment, self-determination and self control with self-indulgent spa treatments!

"Mastering NITs in the Workplace" – here are the keys for creating a major shift in the attitude and outcomes in the workplace, while de-stressing with health spa treatments.

"Pamper, Empower, Enlighten" – a self indulgent pampering retreat while learning the skills for long term empowerment and connecting to your spirituality.

"Eat, Pray, Laugh" - reconnecting with your inner self for relaxation, harnessing the power of your mind and connecting with your higher consciousness. Learn the skills to heal yourself from within.

Customised programs able to be designed on request.

Resources

Video Trailer of "Mastering Negative Impulsive Thoughts" Book

Free Optimism Assessment
Get your optimism score assessed online and see where you are on the scale of positivity!

No NITs toolbox
Get practical tools to use in your personal life or workplace to sharpen your skills in recognising and treating NITs, deal with conflict positively, achieve your ultimate relationship and share the knowledge with others.

Audio CD / MP3 Series

"Golden Steps to Success"
Taking you from where you are now, to where you want to be! Proven, powerful techniques for success in every area of your life. You can do it – and here is the "How"!

"Stress and Anxiety – Taking Control"
Feel stress leave your body as you take control of your mind and find deeper levels of relaxation. Practical strategies and meditation processes that are effective within minutes.

"Depression – Lifting the Cloud"
Feel the clouds lifting and liberate yourself from depression as you listen to the healing tones and accurate medical information to be guided out of the darkness to enjoy life again.

"Discover Relaxation"
First steps to find your paradise of perfect peace and tranquility. Learn to take control of your mind and body to liberate yourself from tension with these guided relaxation exercises.

"Experience Relaxation"
For those with some meditation experience, enjoy deeper levels of relaxation as you are able to control your mind with these beautiful guided meditations.

"Colour Therapy"
Colour to the soul is like vitamins to the body! Enjoy using colour therapy with these guided meditations and sensual, healing tones wash over you and achieve inner peace and tranquility.

Single track audio downloads - also available

Order online at:
www.masteringNITs.com
www.mackaygpsuperclinic.com.au

Acknowledgements

We would like to take the opportunity to acknowledge all of those people in our past that crossed our path and unwittingly or deliberately showed us valuable life lessons that have made this book possible. We sincerely appreciate the many masters, teachers and coaches that imparted their wisdom unselfishly. Also we thank every person that has come to us for personal and professional help over the years, as trusting our wisdom, you followed our advice and with every step you took, our knowledge increased so you were also our valued teachers.

And our greatest teachers of all were those that enabled us to feel great pain and suffering and forced us to strengthen and rebuild ourselves again. So we send them our gratitude for we have benefited from them the most. We send love and blessings to you all.

Our appreciation also goes out to our children for their support, encouragement and belief in us. They are an ongoing source of inspiration as they are already creating their own unique success pathways.

And last, but by no means least, the most amazing, brilliant, generous and considerate partner that each of us have ever had the pleasure of meeting, we thank each other!

John and Elizabeth

Notes...

www.ingramcontent.com/pod-product-compliance
Lightning Source LLC
Chambersburg PA
CBHW070938230426
43666CB00011B/2487